Ages 5 and Up

Alfred's Kid's Ukulele Course
Complete

The Easiest Ukulele Method Ever!

Ron Manus • L. C. Harnsberger

Special thanks to our families, friends, and especially Jennifer, Genevieve, Patrese, and Catherine Harnsberger.

Alfred Music Publishing Co.
P.O. Box 10003
Van Nuys, CA 91410-0003
alfred.com

Copyright © MMXII by Alfred Music Publishing Co., Inc.
All rights reserved. Printed in USA.

No part of this book shall be reproduced, arranged, adapted, recorded, publicly performed, stored in a retrieval system, or transmitted by any means without written permission from the publisher. In order to comply with copyright laws, please apply for such written permission and/or license by contacting the publisher at alfred.com/permissions.

ISBN-10: 0-7390-9366-5 (Book & CD)
ISBN-13: 978-0-7390-9366-5 (Book & CD)

Cover and interior illustrations by Jeff Shelly.
Ukulele photo courtesy of Martin Guitars.
Photos on page 8 by Jennifer Harnsberger Photography.

Contents

Selecting Your Ukulele 5	**The Quarter Rest** 18
Parts of the Ukulele 6	*Three Blind Mice* 18
Caring for Your Ukulele 6	**Activity:** The Quarter Rest 19
Tuning Your Ukulele 7	**The C7 Chord** 20
How to Hold Your Ukulele 8	*My Second Chord* 20
Strumming the Strings 9	**Activity:** The C7 Chord 21
Strumming with a Pick 9	*Troubadour Song* 22
Strumming with Your Fingers 9	**The F Chord** 23
Time to Strum! 9	*My Third Chord* 23
Strumming Notation 10	**Activity:** The F Chord 24
Beats 10	**Three Chords in One Song** 25
Introducing the Quarter-Note Slash 10	*Rain Comes Down* 25
The Staff and Treble Clef 10	*Skip to My Lou* 26
Bar Lines, Measures, and Time Signatures 10	*London Bridge* 27
More Time to Strum 10	**The Repeat Sign** 28
Activity: The Staff and Treble Clef 11	*Merrily We Roll Along* 28
Activity: Bar Lines and Measures 12	**Activity:** The Repeat Sign 29
Activity: The $\frac{4}{4}$ Time Signature 13	*Love Somebody* 30
Activity: The Quarter-Note Slash 13	**The G7 Chord** 31
Activity: Counting Time 14	*My Fourth Chord* 31
Using Your Left Hand 15	**Activity:** The G7 Chord 32
Hand Position 15	**Using G7 with Other Chords** 33
Placing a Finger on a String 15	*A-Tisket, A-Tasket* 34
How to Read Chord Diagrams 15	*Aloha 'Oe (Farewell to Thee)* 35
The C Chord 16	*When the Saints Go Marching In* 36
My First Chord 16	*Yankee Doodle* 37
Activity: The C Chord 17	

An MP3 CD is included that contains all the songs in the book, so you may listen and play along with them. A CD icon beside the title of each song shows the track number. Above each CD icon, the original book number is indicated so that when you access the MP3 tracks, they are conveniently organized by book in separate folders on the disc.

The disc is playable on any CD player or computer equipped to play MP3 CDs. To access the MP3s on your computer, place the CD in your disc drive. In Windows, double-click on My Computer, then right-click on the CD icon labeled "MP3 Files" and select Explore to view the files and copy them to your hard drive. For Mac, double-click on the CD icon on your desktop labeled "MP3 Files" to view the files and copy them to your hard drive.

Activity: Write Your Own Song with Four Chords 38	**The Half Rest** 57
Getting Acquainted with Music Notation 39	*When I Feel Best* 57
Notes 39	**Activity:** The Half Rest 58
The Staff 39	**Notes on the Second String: Introducing G** 59
The Music Alphabet 39	*A-Choo!* 59
Clefs 39	**Activity:** The Note G (2nd String) 60
Activity: The Staff 40	**Activity:** The Notes E, F, G, A, B, and C 61
Introducing the Quarter Note 41	**The Half Note** 62
Clap and Count out Loud 41	*Hot Cross Buns* 62
Activity: The Quarter Note 42	**Activity:** The Half Note 63
Notes on the First String: Introducing A 43	**Notes on the Third String: Introducing C** 64
Abby, the Armadillo 43	*Three Open Strings* 64
Activity: The Note A (1st String) 44	*Little Steps and Big leaps* 64
The Note A with Chords 45	**Activity:** The Note C (3rd String) 65
Note and Strum 45	*The Old Grey Mare* 66
Notes on the First String: Introducing B 46	**Notes on the Third String: Introducing D** 67
Up-Down-Up 46	*D Is Easy!* 67
Activity: The Note B (1st String) 47	*Taking a Walk* 67
The Notes A and B with Chords 48	**Activity:** The Note D (3rd String) 68
Notes on the First String: Introducing C 49	**Activity:** The Whole Note 69
The Mountain Climber 49	**Activity:** Review: All the Notes and Chords in Book 1 69
Activity: The Note C (1st String) 50	*Ode to Joy* 70
The Notes A, B, and C with Chords 51	*Jingle Bells* 71
Brave in the Cave 51	*Mary Had a Little Lamb* 72
Notes on the Second String: Introducing E 52	*Over the Rainbow* 73
Two Open Strings 52	**Music Matching Games** 74
Two-String Melody 52	*All the Notes I Know So Far* 75
Activity: The Note E (2nd String) 53	*This Is an Octave* 75
Jumping Around 54	*Largo* 76
Notes on the Second String: Introducing F 55	**Dotted Half Notes & $\frac{3}{4}$ Time** 77
Ping Pong Song 55	*Three Is for Me!* 77
Soccer Game 55	**Activity:** The Dotted Half Note 78
Activity: The Note F (2nd String) 56	**Activity:** The $\frac{3}{4}$ Time Signature 78

The Farmer in the Dell 79	*Echo Rock* 107
Beautiful Brown Eyes 80	*The Streets of Laredo* 108
Introducing Common Time 81	The Down-and-Up-Stroke 109
Old MacDonald Had a Farm 81	**Activity:** Dynamics 110
Activity: Common Time 82	**Activity:** The Downstroke and Upstroke 110
Introducing B-Flat 83	The Fermata 111
Aura Lee 83	*Michael, Row the Boat Ashore* 111
Activity: The Note B-flat 84	**Activity:** The Fermata 112
Three-String Boogie 85	Introducing F-Sharp 113
Tempo Signs 86	*Little Brown Jug* 113
Three-Tempo Rock 86	**Activity:** The Note F-sharp 114
Rockin' Uke 87	The G Chord 115
Good Night Ladies 88	The D7 Chord 115
Blues in C 89	*Over the Rainbow (Extended Version)* 116
Ties 90	**Activity:** The G and D7 Chords 118
Down in the Valley 90	**Activity:** Review: All the Notes and Chords You Learned in Books 1 & 2 119
Activity: Ties 92	**Music Matching Games** 120
Key Signatures 93	
Ode to Joy (Extended Version) 93	
Activity: Key Signatures 94	
Pickup Measures 95	
A-Tisket, A-Tasket 95	
Activity: Pickup Measures 96	
Tom Dooley 97	
Eighth Notes 98	
Jammin' with Eighth Notes 98	
Activity: The Eighth Note 99	
Go Tell Aunt Rhody 100	
Love Somebody (Extended Version) 101	
Clementine 102	
Dotted Quarter Notes 104	
Counting Dotted Quarter Notes 104	
Cockles and Mussels 104	
Activity: The Dotted Quarter Note 106	
Dynamics 107	

Selecting Your Ukulele

Ukuleles come in different types and sizes. There are four basic sizes: soprano, concert, tenor, and baritone. The smallest is the soprano, and they get gradually bigger, with the baritone being the largest.

Soprano **Concert** **Tenor** **Baritone**

Soprano, concert, and tenor ukes are all tuned to the same notes, but the baritone is tuned to different notes. Each uke has a different sound. The soprano has a light, soft sound, which is what you expect when you hear a ukulele. The larger the instrument, the deeper the sound is. Some tenor ukuleles have six or even eight strings.

The soprano ukulele is the most common, but you can use soprano, concert, and four-string tenor ukuleles with this book. Because the baritone uke is tuned to the same notes as the top four strings of the guitar, you can use *Alfred's Kid's Guitar Method Book 1* to start learning on that type of ukulele.

Parts of the Ukulele

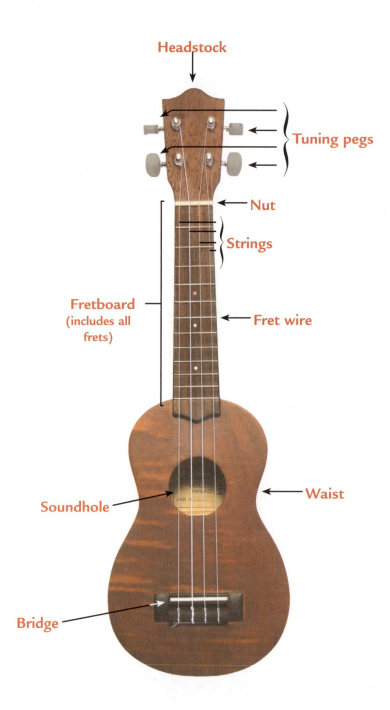

Caring for Your Ukulele

Get to know your ukulele and treat it like a friend. When you carry it, think of it as part of your body so you don't accidentally bump it against walls or furniture, and be especially sure not to drop it! Every time you are done playing, carefully dust off your ukulele with a soft cloth, and be sure to put it away in its case. If you don't have a case, always put it in a safe place where it won't be in the way.

Tuning Your Ukulele

First make sure your strings are wound properly around the tuning pegs. They should go from the inside to the outside, as in the picture.

Turning a tuning peg clockwise makes the pitch lower. Turning a tuning peg counter-clockwise makes the pitch higher. Be sure not to tune the strings too high because they could break!

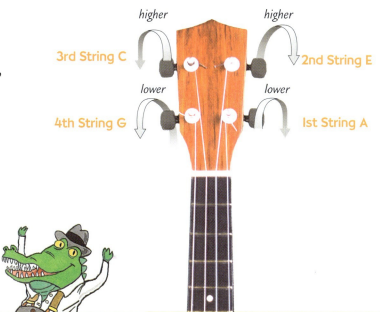

Important:
Always remember that the string closest to the floor is the first string. The one closest to the ceiling is the fourth string.

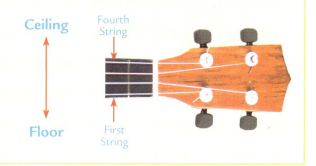

Book 1
Tracks 1 & 2

Tuning with the MP3 CD
Using Your CD
Put the CD in your CD player or computer (see page 2) and play Tracks 1 and 2. Listen to the directions and match each of your ukulele's strings to its pitch on the CD.

Tuning without the MP3 CD

Tuning the Ukulele to Itself
When your first string is in tune, you can tune the rest of the strings just using the ukulele alone. First tune the first string to A on the piano, then follow the instructions to the right to get the ukulele in tune.

Press fret 5 of string 2 and tune it to the pitch of string 1 (A).

Press fret 4 of string 3 and tune it to the pitch of string 2 (E).

Press fret 2 of string 4 and tune it to the pitch of string 1 (A).

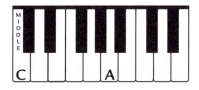

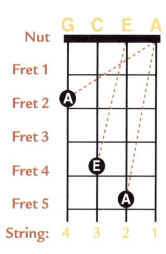

Pitch Pipes and Electronic Tuners
If you don't have a piano available, buying an electronic tuner or pitch pipe is recommended. The salesperson at your music store can show you how to use them.

How to Hold Your Ukulele

Hold your ukulele in the position that is most comfortable for you. Some positions are shown below.

Sitting

Rest the ukulele gently on your thigh.

Cradle the ukulele with your right arm by gently holding it close to your body. Your right hand should be free to strum it.

Standing

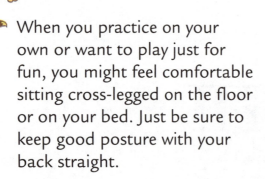

When you practice on your own or want to play just for fun, you might feel comfortable sitting cross-legged on the floor or on your bed. Just be sure to keep good posture with your back straight.

Sitting on the floor

Strumming the Strings

To *strum* means to play the strings with your right hand by brushing quickly across them. There are two common ways of strumming the strings. One is with a pick, and the second is with the fingers.

Strumming with a Pick

Hold the pick between your thumb and index finger. Hold it firmly, but don't squeeze it too hard.

Strum from the fourth string (closest to the ceiling) to the first string (closest to the floor).

Start near the top string.

Move mostly your wrist, not just your arm. Finish near the bottom string.

Strumming with Your Fingers

First decide if you feel more comfortable strumming with the side of your thumb or the nail of your index finger. The strumming motion is the same with the thumb or finger as it is when using the pick. Strum from the fourth string (closest to the ceiling) to the first string (closest to the floor).

Strumming with the thumb

Strumming with the index finger

Important:
Strum by mostly moving your wrist, not just your arm. Use as little motion as possible. Start as close to the top string as you can, and never let your hand move past the edge of the ukulele.

Time to Strum!

Book 1 Track 3

Strum all four strings slowly and evenly.
Count your strums out loud as you play.
Repeat this exercise until you feel comfortable strumming the strings.

strum	strum	strum	strum	strum	strum	strum	strum
/	/	/	/	/	/	/	/
Count: 1	2	3	4	5	6	7	8

Strumming Notation

Beats

Each strum you play is equal to one *beat*. Beats are even, like the ticking of a clock.

tick - tick - tick - tick
beat-beat-beat-beat

Introducing the Quarter-Note Slash

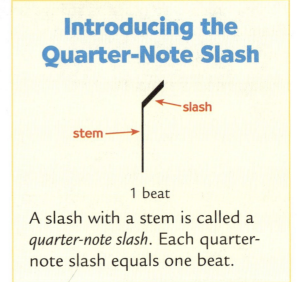

1 beat

A slash with a stem is called a *quarter-note slash*. Each quarter-note slash equals one beat.

The Staff and Treble Clef

Ukulele music is usually written on a five-line *staff* that has a *treble clef* at its beginning.

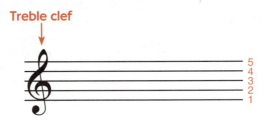

Bar Lines, Measures, and Time Signatures

Bar lines divide the staff into equal parts called measures. A *double bar line* is used at the end to show you the music is finished.

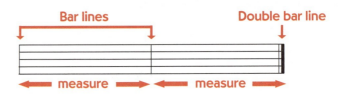

Measures are always filled with a certain number of beats. You know how many beats are in each measure by looking at the *time signature*, which is always at the beginning of the music. A 4/4 time signature ("four-four time") means there are 4 equal beats in every measure.

Book 1
Track 4

More Time to Strum

Play this example in 4/4 time. It will sound the same as "Time to Strum," which you played on the previous page. Keep the beats even and count out loud.

Strum all four strings as you did before.

Strumming all four strings

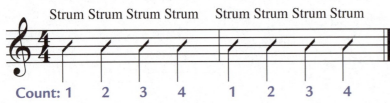

Strum Strum Strum Strum   Strum Strum Strum Strum

Count: 1   2   3   4   1   2   3   4

10

ACTIVITY: The Staff and Treble Clef

Ukulele music is usually written on a five-line *staff*. The lines are numbered from the bottom up.

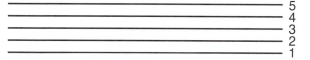

At the beginning of each staff is a *treble clef* that looks like this:

How to Draw the Treble Clef

Step 1: Draw a circle under the staff and fill it in.

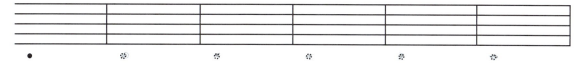

Step 2: Draw a curved line (like the letter "u") that starts from the bottom of the circle and touches the bottom of the first line of the staff.

Step 3: Draw a line up from the first line to the fifth line.

Step 4: Draw a loop above the second line of the staff.

Step 5: Draw a long curving line that goes around the second line of the staff.

Now, draw six treble clefs below.

ACTIVITY: Bar Lines and Measures

Bar lines divide the staff into equal parts called *measures*. A *double bar line* is used at the end to show you the music is finished.

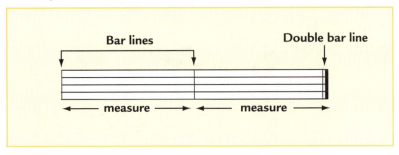

How to Draw Measures

Draw bar lines and a double bar line.

Draw the treble clef, bar lines, and double bar line to make four measures.

Make the same four measures again.

ACTIVITY:
The 4/4 Time Signature

A *time signature* tells you how many beats are in a measure.
A 4/4 time signature means there are four equal beats in every measure.

How to Draw the 4/4 Time Signature

Step 1: Draw a number "4" sitting on top of the third line of the staff.

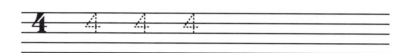

Step 2: Draw a second "4" below the first one, sitting on the bottom line.

Now, draw six 4/4 time signatures.

ACTIVITY:
The Quarter-Note Slash

A slash with a stem is called a *quarter-note slash*.
Each quarter-note slash equals one beat.

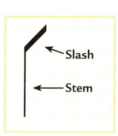

How to Draw the Quarter-Note Slash

Step 1: Create the slash by drawing a slanted line from the second staff line to the fourth staff line.

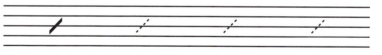

Step 2: Create the stem by drawing a line from the bottom of the slash to just below the staff.

Now, draw six quarter-note slashes.

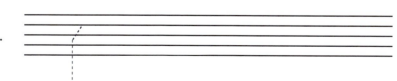

13

ACTIVITY: Counting Time

Draw four quarter-note slashes in each measure.

Write the counts for each measure below the quarter-note slashes.

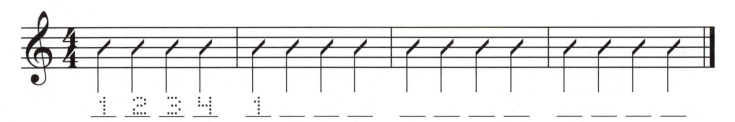

Draw four measures including a treble clef, 4/4 time signature, bar lines, a double bar line, and four quarter-note slashes in each measure. Then, write the counts below the measures.

Using Your Left Hand

Hand Position

Learning to use your left-hand fingers easily starts with a good hand position. Place your hand so your thumb rests comfortably in the middle of the back of the neck. Position your fingers on the front of the neck as if you are gently squeezing a ball between them and your thumb. Keep your elbow in and your fingers curved.

Keep elbow in and fingers curved

Like gently squeezing a ball between your fingertips and thumb

Placing a Finger on a String

When you press a string with a left-hand finger, make sure you press firmly with the tip of your finger and as close to the fret wire as you can without actually being right on it. Short fingernails are important! This will create a clean, bright tone.

RIGHT
Finger presses the string down near the fret without actually being on it.

WRONG
Finger is too far from fret wire; tone is "buzzy" and indefinite.

WRONG
Finger is on top of fret wire; tone is muffled and unclear.

How to Read Chord Diagrams

Chord diagrams show where to place your fingers. The example to the right shows finger 1 on the first string at the first fret. The "o"s above the second, third and fourth strings tell you these strings are to be played open, meaning without pressing down on them with a left-hand finger.

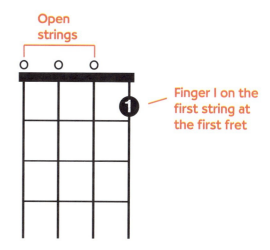

Finger 1 on the first string at the first fret

The C Chord

Hear this chord! Book 1 Track 5

Use finger 3 to press the 1st string at the 3rd fret. If you have any trouble holding finger 3 down to play the C chord, place fingers 1 and 2 on the 1st and 2nd frets behind finger 3 until you are able to play with just finger 3.

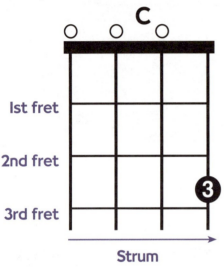

Strumming

Strum the four-string C chord on each quarter-note slash ⁄. Make sure your strums are even. Count aloud as you play:

1-2-3-4 | 1-2-3-4.

Listen to the song on the recording to hear how it should sound!

My First Chord

Book 1 Track 6

Remember: This means there are 4 beats in each measure.

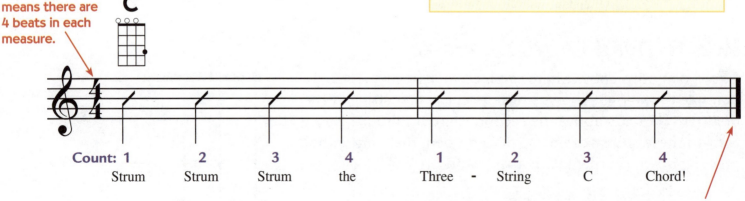

Count: 1 2 3 4 | 1 2 3 4
Strum Strum Strum the Three - String C Chord!

This **double bar line** tells us the music is finished.

16

ACTIVITY: The C Chord

Chord Diagrams

When reading a chord diagram, you will see exactly where to put your fingers. Each vertical line represents one of the four strings of the ukulele: from left to right, 4 3 2 1. An **o** above a string means it is played open (not fingered). A circled number on a string shows you which finger to use and where to place it on that string.

C Chord

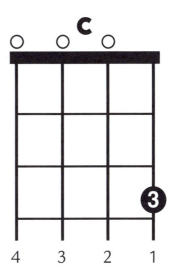

Strings: 4 3 2 1

Write the chord symbol "C" three times.

Draw the **o**'s and fingering for the C chords below.

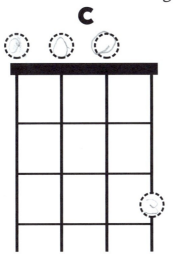

The Quarter Rest

Introducing the Quarter Rest

1 beat

This strange-looking music symbol means to be silent for one beat. Stop the sound of the strings by lightly touching them with the side of your hand, as in the photo.

Book 1 Track 7

Rest Warm-up

Before playing "Three Blind Mice," practice this exercise until you are comfortable playing rests.

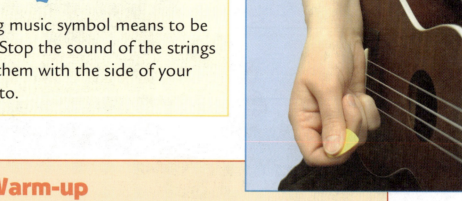

Practice Tip

Strum the chords and have a friend sing the words.

Three Blind Mice

Book 1 Track 8

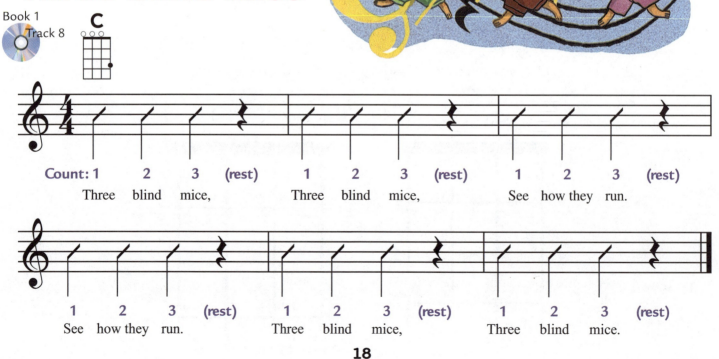

ACTIVITY: The Quarter Rest

The *quarter rest* means to be silent for one beat.

How to Draw the Quarter Rest

Step 1: Draw a short line slanting down from left to right.

Step 2: Draw a longer line slanting down from right to left starting at the bottom of the first line.

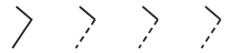

Step 3: Draw another short line slanting down from left to right starting at the bottom of the second line.

Step 4: Draw a curled line, almost like a letter "c," starting at the bottom of the third line.

Now, draw five quarter rests.

Counting Time

Fill in the missing beats with quarter rests.

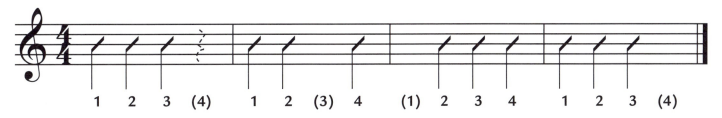

      1   2   3 (4)   1   2 (3) 4   (1) 2   3   4   1   2   3 (4)

Write the counts below the staff. Put parentheses around the counts that are for rests.

      1   2   3 (4)

19

The C⁷ Chord

Use finger 1 to press the 1st string at the 1st fret. This chord is just like the C chord but you are using your 1st finger and not your 3rd finger.

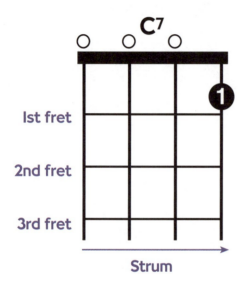

My Second Chord

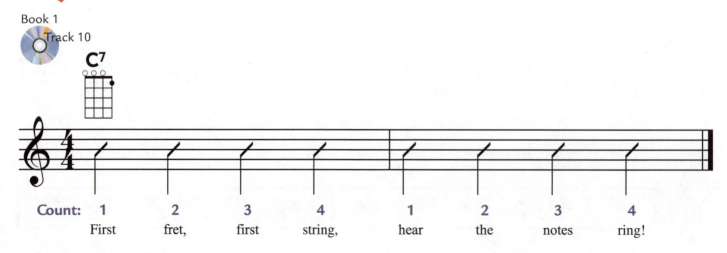

Count: 1   2   3   4   1   2   3   4
       First fret, first string, hear the notes ring!

ACTIVITY: The C⁷ Chord

The C⁷ Chord

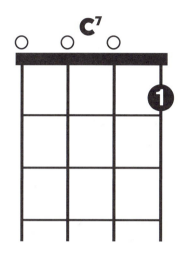

Finish drawing the **o**'s and fingering for the chords below.

Write the chord symbol "C⁷" three times.

Troubadour Song

Remember to stop the sound by lightly touching the strings with the side of your hand on each 𝄽. Wait one beat.

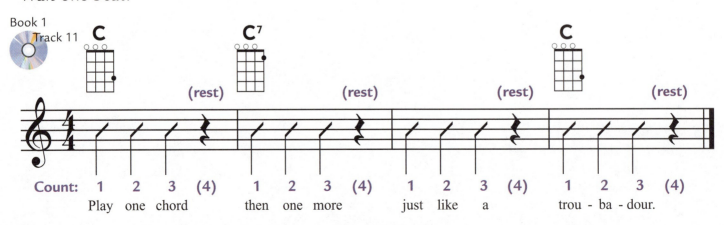

*A troubadour was a musician who traveled around singing and playing.

The F Chord

Hear this chord!
Book 1
Track 12

This is the first time you are pressing two fingers down at one time. First press finger 1 on the 2nd string at the 1st fret. Then use finger 2 to press the 4th string at the 2nd fret. Press both fingers down firmly as you strum all the strings.

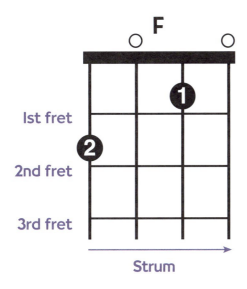

My Third Chord

Book 1
Track 13

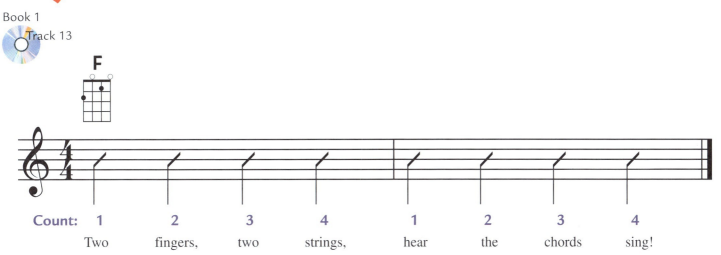

Count: 1   2   3   4   1   2   3   4
Two fingers, two strings, hear the chords sing!

ACTIVITY: The F Chord

The F Chord

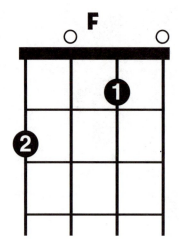

Finish drawing the o's and fingering for the chords below.

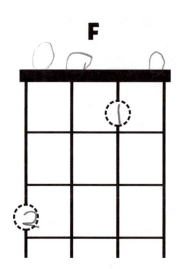

Write the chord symbol "F" three times.

F
F
F

Three Chords in One Song

F    **C⁷** 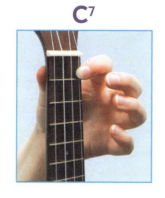   **C**

Remember: This song has three different chords in it. At first, take your time and play slowly so that all the notes sound clearly. Don't forget to be silent for a beat on each quarter rest as you change to a new chord.

Rain Comes Down

Book 1, Track 14

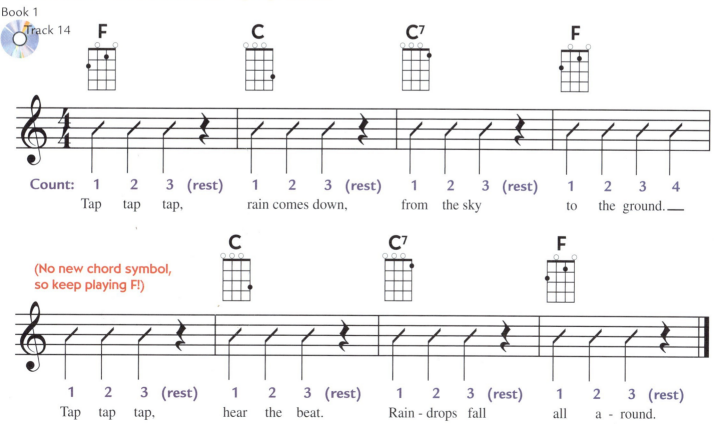

(No new chord symbol, so keep playing F!)

Skip to My Lou

C⁷ **F** **C**

Practice Tip
To change quickly from C⁷ to F in the last two measures, move your 1st finger to the 2nd string—that's not very far—and then put your 2nd finger on the 4th string.

Book 1 Track 15

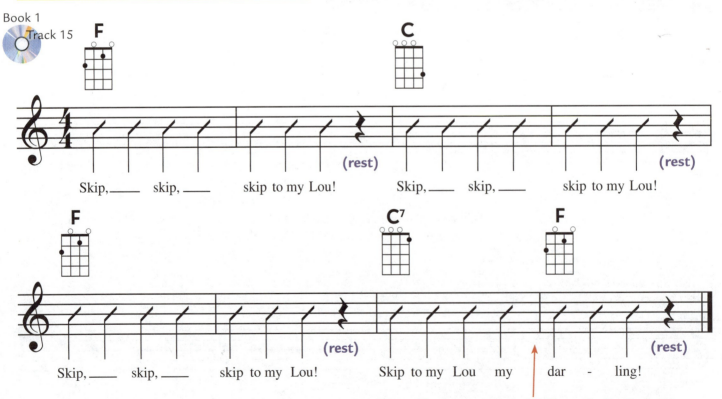

Skip,___ skip,___ skip to my Lou! Skip,___ skip,___ skip to my Lou!

Skip,___ skip,___ skip to my Lou! Skip to my Lou my dar - ling!

Remember to move your 1st finger to the 2nd string and then put your 2nd finger on the 4th string to play the F chord on the next beat.

26

London Bridge

Book 1
Track 16

F   **C**   **F**

(rest)   (rest)   (rest)

Lon - don Bridge is   fal - ling down,   fal - ling down,   fal - ling down

C⁷   **F**

(No new chord symbol, so keep playing F!)

(rest)   (rest)

Lon - don Bridge is   fal - ling down,   my___ fair___ la - dy.

The Repeat Sign

Introducing Repeat Dots :|

Double dots on the inside of a double bar line mean to go back to the beginning and play again.

Merrily We Roll Along

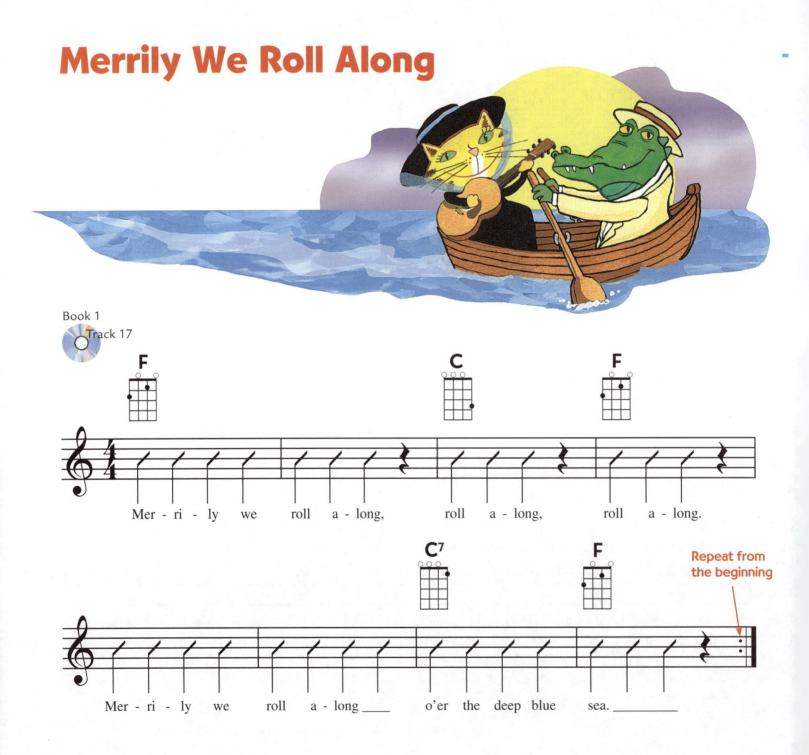

ACTIVITY: The Repeat Sign

When *double dots* are written on the inside of a double bar line, it makes a *repeat sign*. A repeat sign means to go back to the beginning and play the same music again.

How to Draw the Repeat Sign

Draw repeat signs by adding double dots to these double bar lines.

Draw a double bar line above each "Don't Repeat," and draw a repeat sign above each "Repeat."

Repeat   **Don't Repeat**   **Repeat**   **Repeat**   **Don't Repeat**

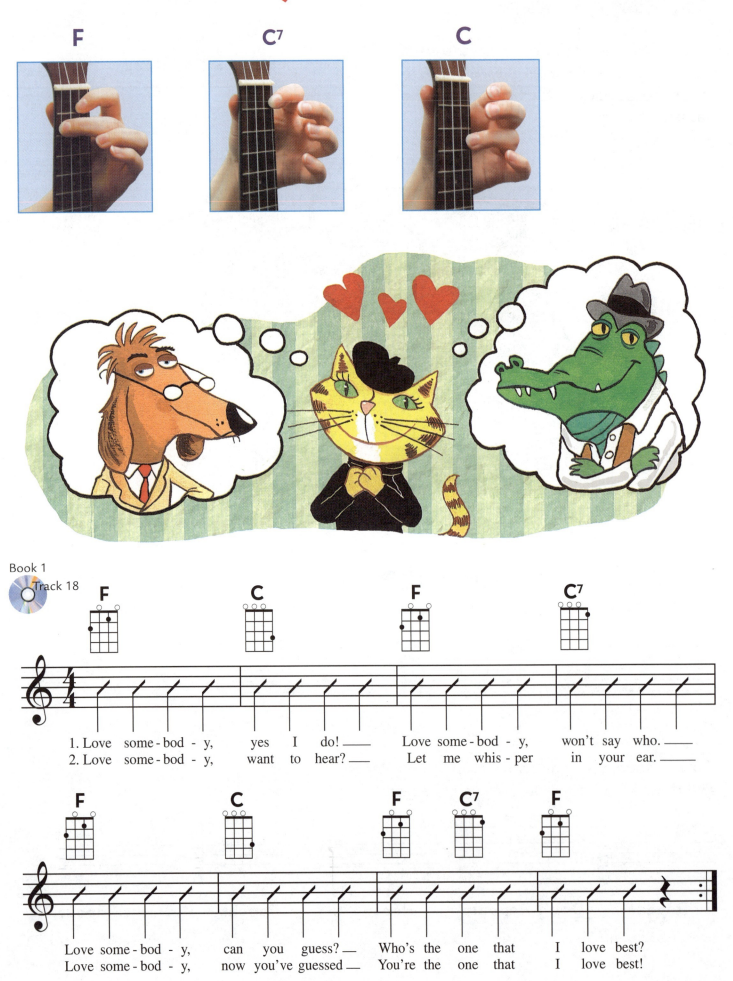

The G⁷ Chord

Hear this chord! Book 1 Track 19

Use finger 1 to press the 2nd string at the 1st fret. Use fingers 2 and 3 to press the 3rd and 1st strings at the 2nd fret.

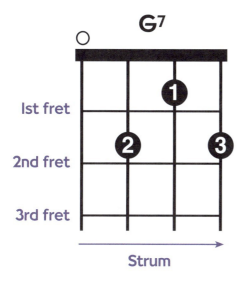

My Fourth Chord

Book 1 Track 20

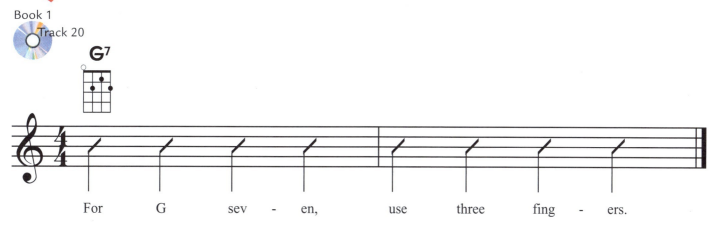

For G sev-en, use three fing-ers.

ACTIVITY: The G⁷ Chord

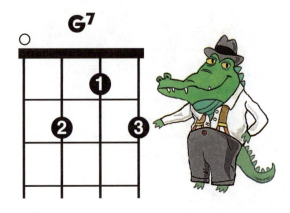

Write the chord symbol "G⁷" three times.

Draw the **o**'s for these chords.

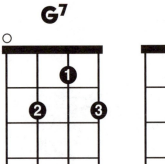   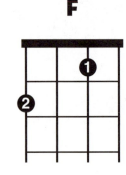

Let's Practice Writing Music

Finish creating four measures of music by tracing the treble clefs, time signature, bar lines, quarter-note slashes, quarter rests, repeat sign, and chord frames.

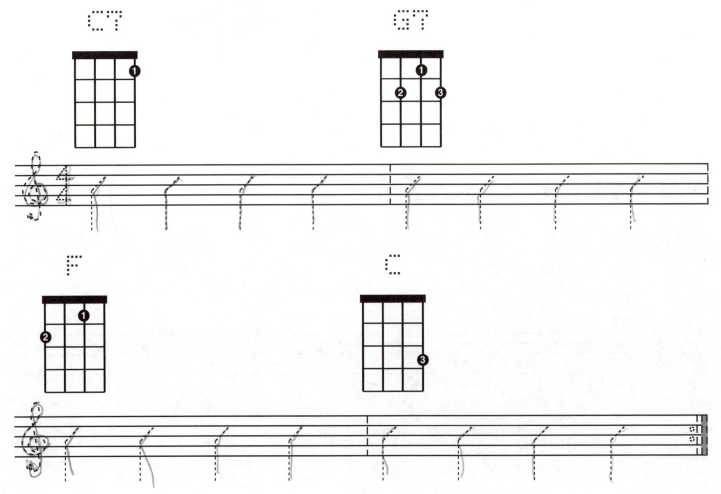

32

Using G7 with Other Chords

> **Practice Tip**
>
> Before you play "A-Tisket, A-Tasket," "Aloha 'Oe," "When the Saints Go Marching In," and "Yankee Doodle," practice the exercises on this page. They will help you to change chords easily.
>
> Play each exercise very slowly at first, and gradually play them faster. Don't move on to play the songs until you can easily move from chord to chord without missing a beat.

Book 1 Track 21
No. 1

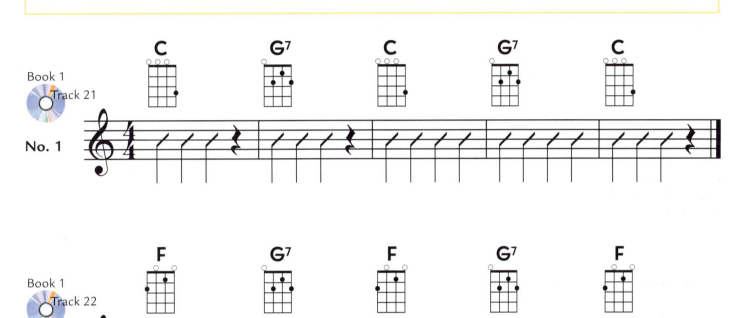

Book 1 Track 22
No. 2

Book 1 Track 23
No. 3

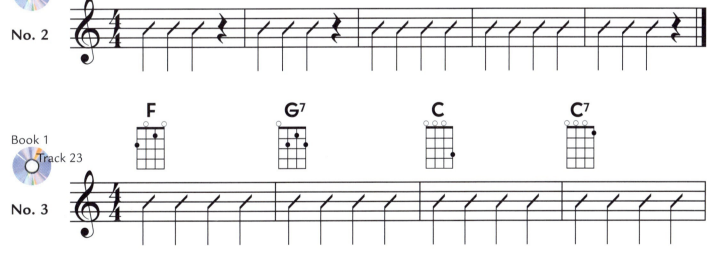

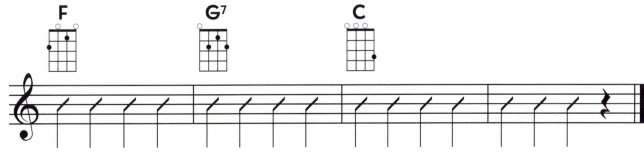

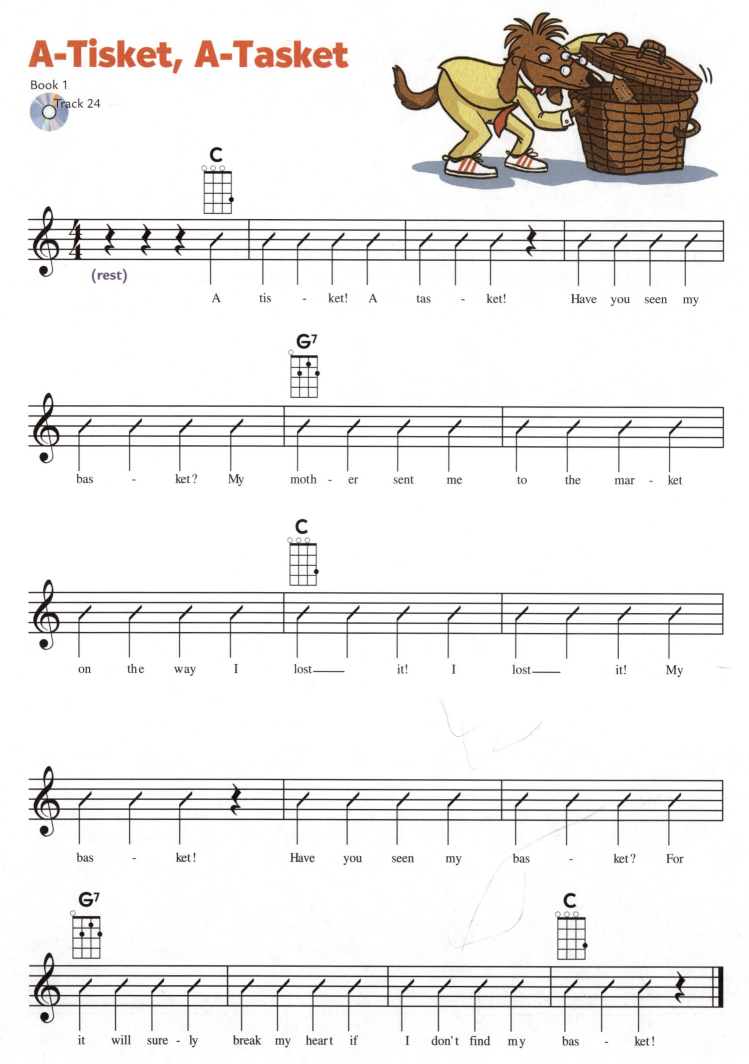

Aloha 'Oe (Farewell to Thee)

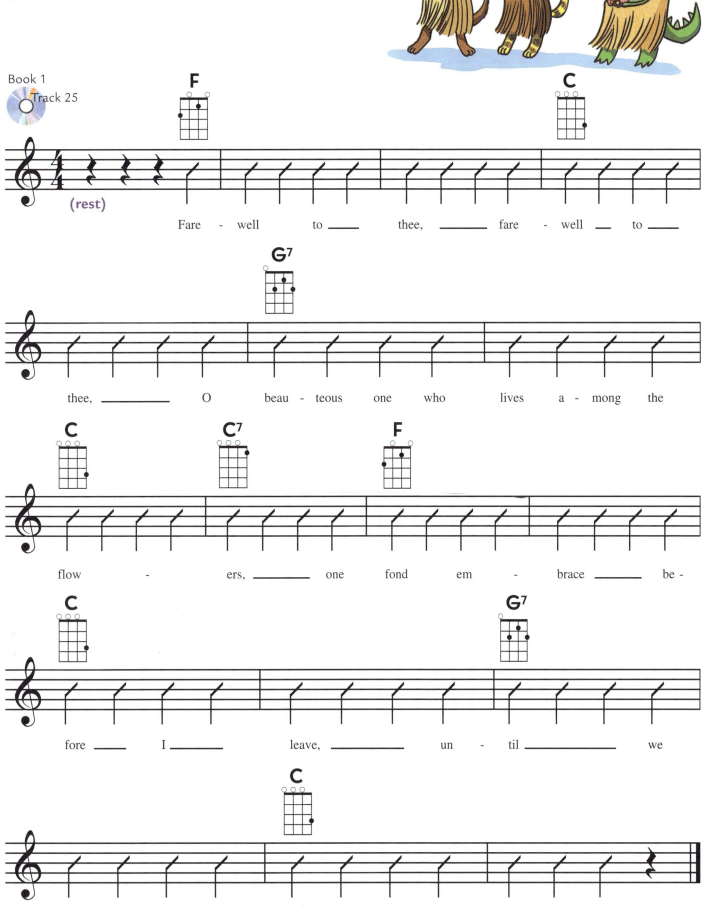

When the Saints Go Marching In

Yankee Doodle

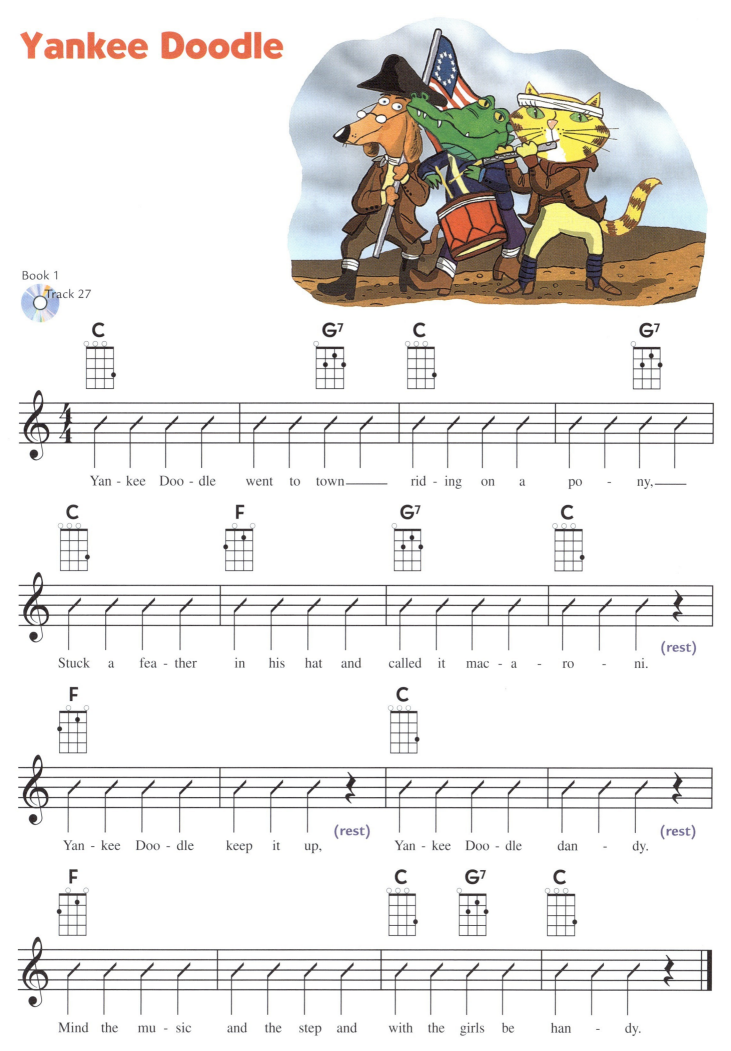

Book 1
Track 27

Yan - kee Doo - dle went to town ___ rid - ing on a po - ny, ___
Stuck a fea - ther in his hat and called it mac - a - ro - ni. (rest)
Yan - kee Doo - dle keep it up, (rest) Yan - kee Doo - dle dan - dy. (rest)
Mind the mu - sic and the step and with the girls be han - dy.

ACTIVITY: Write Your Own Song with Four Chords

Here's your chance to write your first song. Follow these steps.
1. Draw a treble clef at the beginning of each staff.
2. Draw a $\frac{4}{4}$ time signature next to the treble clef in the first measure.
3. Fill in the bar lines and draw a repeat sign at the end.
4. Draw quarter-note slashes and quarter rests. You can choose which beats have slashes and which have rests, but be sure there are exactly four beats in each measure.
5. Choose which chords you want by filling in the chord frame above each measure.
6. Make up your own lyrics and write them below each staff.
7. **Have fun** and play your song on your ukulele.

Getting Acquainted with Music Notation

Notes

Musical sounds are represented by symbols called *notes*. Their time value is determined by their color (black or white), and by stems and flags attached to them.

The Staff

Each note has a name. That name depends on where the note is found on the *staff*. The staff is made up of five horizontal lines and the spaces between those lines.

The Music Alphabet

The notes are named after the first seven letters of the alphabet (A–G).

Clefs

As music notation progressed through history, the staff had from two to twenty lines, and symbols were invented that would always give you a reference point for all the other notes. These symbols were called *clefs*.

Music for the ukulele is written in the G or *treble clef*. Originally, the Gothic letter G was used on a four-line staff to show the pitch G.

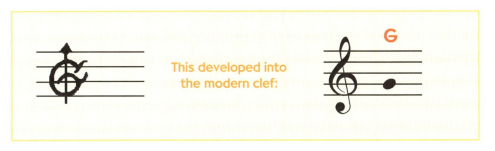

This developed into the modern clef:

39

ACTIVITY: The Staff

The *staff* is made up of five horizontal lines and the four spaces between those lines. The lines and spaces are numbered from the bottom up.

Name the line or space for each note.

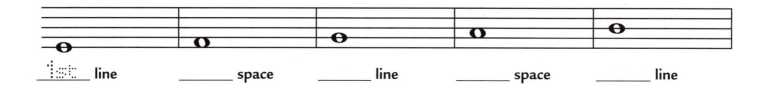

_1st_ line   _____ space   _____ line   _____ space   _____ line

_____ space   _____ line   _____ space   _____ line

Name the line for each note in the box below the staff.

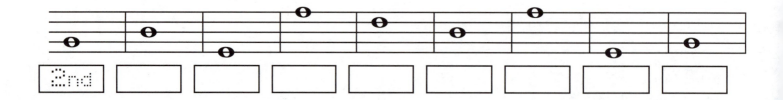

| 2nd | | | | | | | | |

Name the space for each note in the box below the staff.

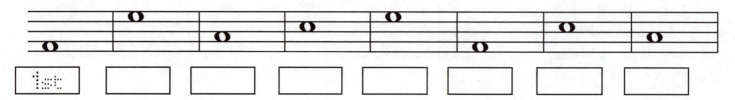

| 1st | | | | | | | |

40

An easy way to remember the notes on the lines is using the phrase **E**very **G**ood **B**ird **D**oes **F**ly. Remembering the notes in the spaces is even easier because they spell the word **FACE**, which rhymes with "space."

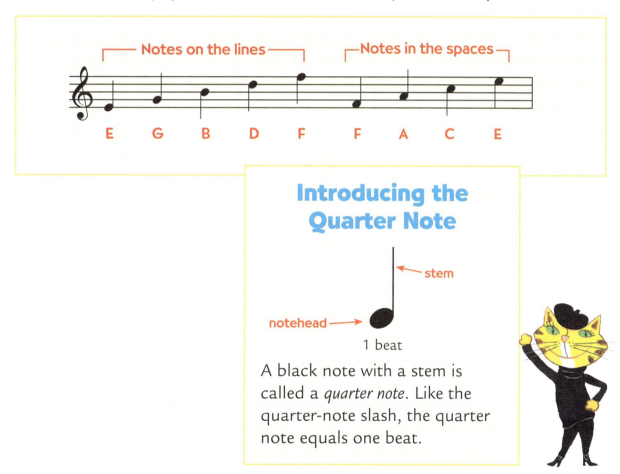

Introducing the Quarter Note

A black note with a stem is called a *quarter note*. Like the quarter-note slash, the quarter note equals one beat.

Book 1
Track 28

Clap and Count out Loud

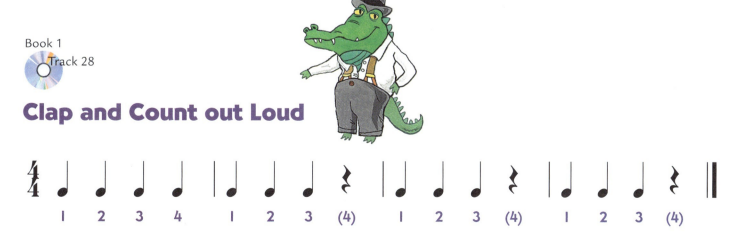

41

ACTIVITY: The Quarter Note

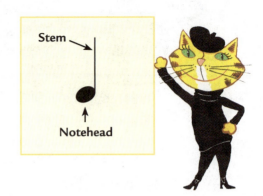

A *quarter note* has a black notehead and a stem. Each quarter note equals one beat.

How to Draw the Quarter Note

Step 1: To create the notehead, draw an oval and fill it in. Draw several noteheads below in the third space.

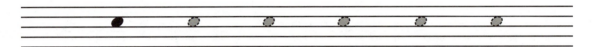

Step 2: To create the stem, draw a line going down from the left of the notehead to just below the staff.

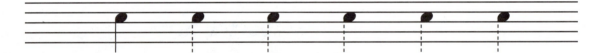

Now, draw six quarter notes on the third space of the staff.

Now, draw six quarter notes in the second space with the stem going up from the right of the notehead.

Counting Time

Draw four quarter notes in each measure. In the first two measures, draw quarter notes having stems down, and in the second two measures, draw quarter notes having stems up. Then, write the counts below the staff.

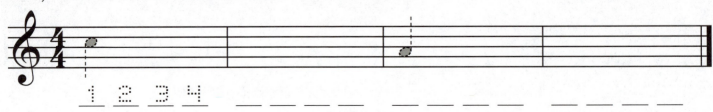

1 2 3 4

Notes on the First String
Introducing A

A note sitting on the second space of the treble clef staff is called A. To play this note, pick the open 1st string (meaning without putting a left-hand finger on it).

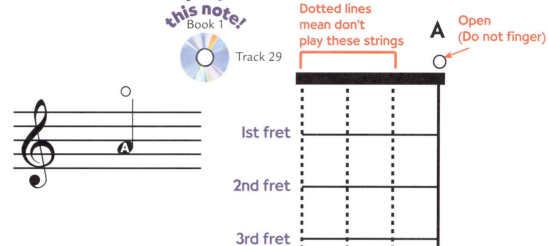

Hear this note!
Book 1
Track 29

Dotted lines mean don't play these strings

A — Open (Do not finger)

1st fret
2nd fret
3rd fret

Abby, the Armadillo

Book 1
Track 30

Picking
- Play each A slowly and evenly, using a *downpick* motion. We will use only downpicks for the rest of the book.
- Use only a little motion to pick each note, just like strumming.

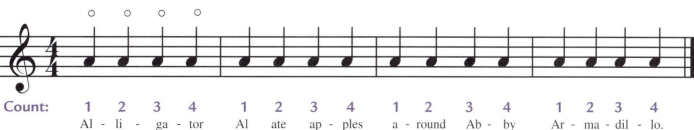

Count: 1 2 3 4 | 1 2 3 4 | 1 2 3 4 | 1 2 3 4
Al - li - ga - tor   Al ate ap - ples   a - round Ab - by   Ar - ma - dil - lo.

43

ACTIVITY: The Note A (1st String)

The note on the second space of the staff is called A.

Drawing the Note A

Step 1: Draw an oval notehead in the second space of the staff.

Step 2: For the stem, draw a line from the right of the notehead to just above the top line of the staff. The stem always goes up for this note.

Now, draw the note A six times below.

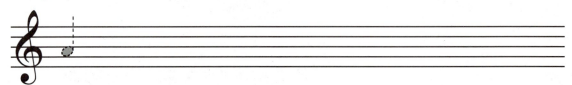

Playing the Note A

To play the note A, pick the open 1st string.

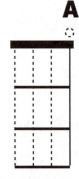

Indicate the fingering for note A by placing "**o**" above the 1st string on each diagram.

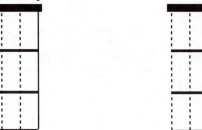
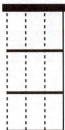

The Note A with Chords

Practice Tip

For this tune, remember that both the F and C⁷ chords use finger 1 at the 1st fret.

F Chord   **C⁷ Chord**

It's easy to move your finger over one string to change chords, but don't forget your 2nd finger on the 4th string.

Book 1 Track 31

Note and Strum Warm-up

Before playing "Note and Strum" practice this exercise slowly until you are comfortable playing a note followed by a strum.

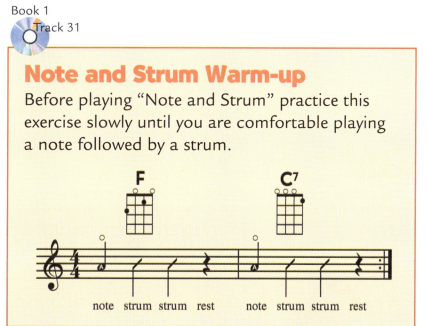

Note and Strum

Book 1 Track 32

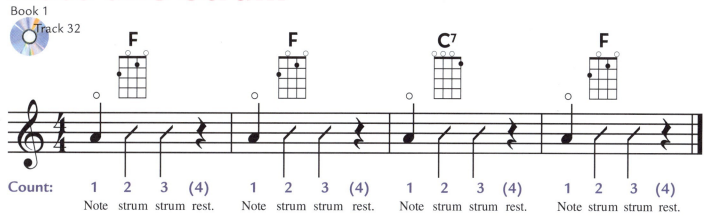

Notes on the First String
Introducing B

A note on the middle line of the staff is called B. To play this note, use finger 2 to press the 1st string at the 2nd fret. Use a downpick motion to play only the 1st string.

Hear this note!
Book 1 — Track 33

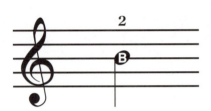

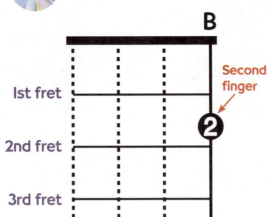

Book 1 — Track 34

Up-Down-Up Warm-up

Before playing "Up-Down-Up," practice this exercise until you are comfortable playing the note B.

Up-Down-Up

Book 1 — Track 35

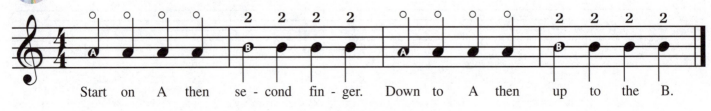

Start on A then se - cond fin - ger. Down to A then up to the B.

46

ACTIVITY: The Note B (1st String)

The note on the middle line of the staff is called B.

Drawing the Note B

Step 1: Draw an oval notehead on the second line of the staff.

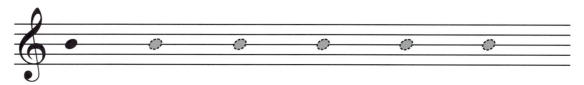

Step 2: For the stem, draw a line from the left of the notehead to just below the bottom line of the staff. The stem always goes down for this note.

Now, draw the note B six times below.

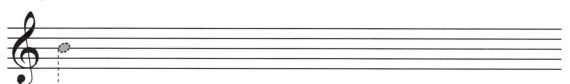

Playing the Note B

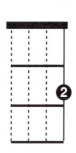

To play the note B, press the 2nd fret of the 1st string.

Indicate the fingering for note B by placing the number "2" in a circle on the 2nd fret of the 1st string on each diagram.

47

The Notes A and B with Chords

Practice Tip

For this tune, notice that the note B and the C chord are one finger apart. Finger the B with the 2nd finger on the 2nd fret of the 1st string, and then use the 3rd finger on the 3rd fret of the 1st string to play the C chord. First, just practice switching those fingers and then play the music below.

Note B

C Chord

Book 1
Track 36

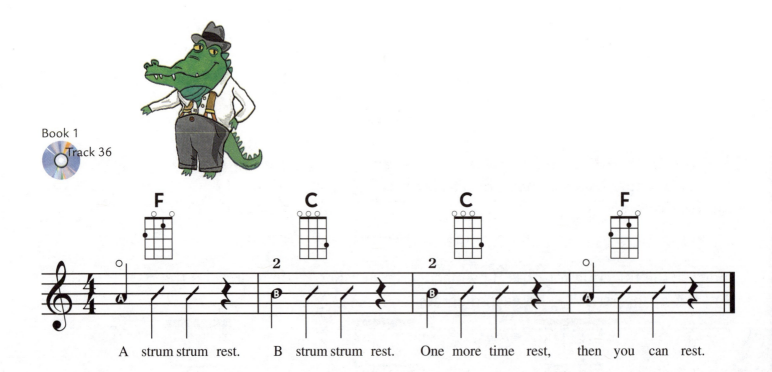

Notes on the First String
Introducing C

Hear this note!
Book 1 Track 37

A note sitting on the third space of the treble clef staff is called C. Use finger 3 to press the 1st string at the 3rd fret. Use a downpick motion to play only the 1st string.

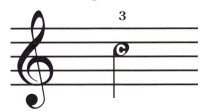
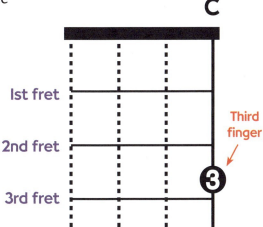

Book 1 Track 38

C Warm-up

The Mountain Climber

Book 1 Track 39

From the bot-tom to the top, the fear-less climb-er does not stop.

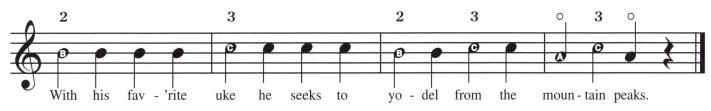

With his fav-'rite uke he seeks to yo-del from the moun-tain peaks.

ACTIVITY: The Note C (1st String)

The note on the third space of the staff is called C.

Drawing the Note C

Step 1: Draw an oval notehead on the third space of the staff.

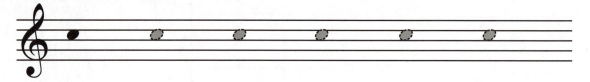

Step 2: For the stem, draw a line from the left of the notehead to just below the bottom line of the staff. The stem always goes down for this note.

Now, draw the note C six times below.

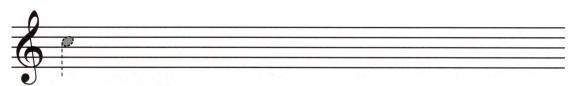

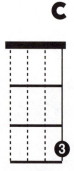

Playing the Note C

To play the note C, press the 3rd fret of the 1st string.

Indicate the fingering for note C by placing the number "3" in a circle on the 3rd fret of the 1st string on each diagram.

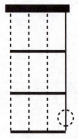 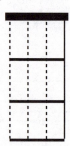 

The Notes A, B, and C with Chords

> **Practice Tip**
>
> Notice that the note C and the C chord are both fingered with finger 3 at the 3rd fret on the 1st string.
>
>
>
> **Note C**   **C Chord**
>
> Hold down the 3rd finger between the note C and the C chord.

Brave in the Cave

Book 1
Track 40

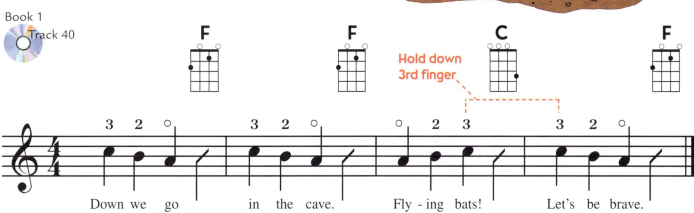

Down we go in the cave. Fly-ing bats! Let's be brave.

51

Notes on the Second String
Introducing E

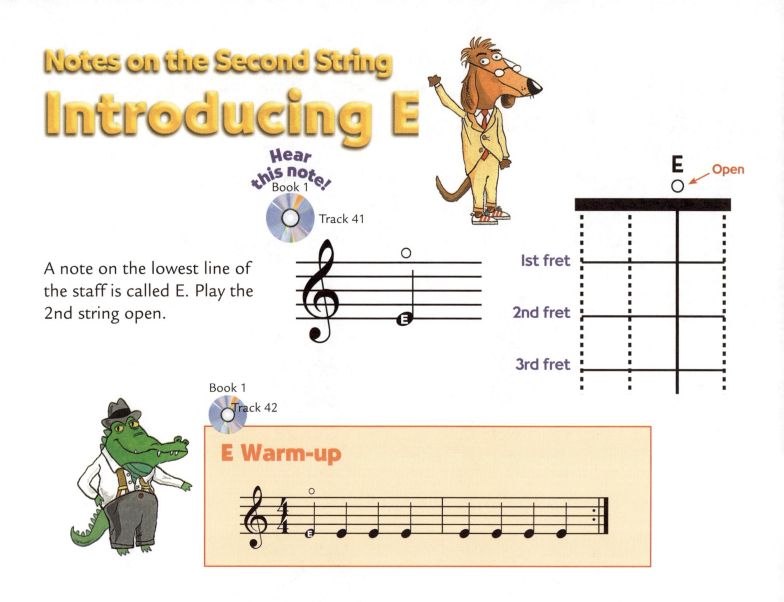

A note on the lowest line of the staff is called E. Play the 2nd string open.

Two Open Strings

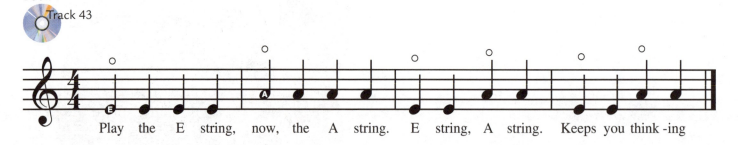

Play the E string, now, the A string. E string, A string. Keeps you think-ing

Two-String Melody

Notes on two strings are fun to play. Notes on two strings, Oh! what fun!

ACTIVITY: The Note E (2nd String)

The note on the bottom line of the staff is called E.

Drawing the Note E

Step 1: Draw an oval notehead on the first line of the staff.

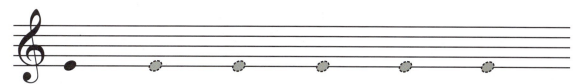

Step 2: For the stem, draw a line from the right of the notehead to just below the top line of the staff. The stem always goes up for this note.

Now, draw the note E six times below.

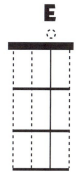

Playing the Note E

To play the note E, pick the open 2nd string.

Indicate the fingering for note E by placing "**o**" above the 2nd string on each diagram.

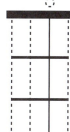 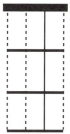 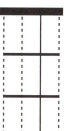

Jumping Around

Book 1
Track 45

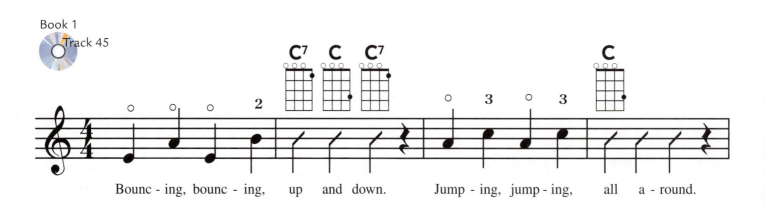

Bounc-ing, bounc-ing, up and down. Jump-ing, jump-ing, all a-round.

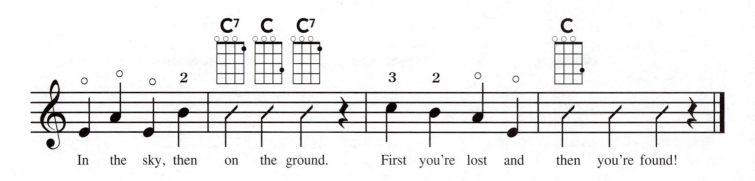

In the sky, then on the ground. First you're lost and then you're found!

Notes on the Second String
Introducing F

Hear this note!
Book 1 Track 46

A note on the 1st space of the staff is called F. Use finger 1 to press the 2nd string at the 1st fret. Pick only the 2nd string.

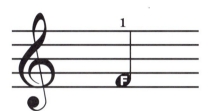
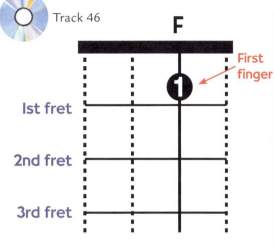

Book 1 Track 47

F Warm-up

Ping Pong Song

Book 1 Track 48

O - pen E string, first fin - ger F, down to E then up to F.

Soccer Game

Book 1 Track 49

Hold

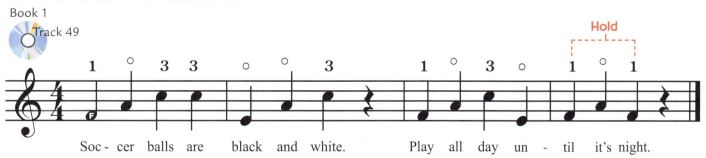

Soc - cer balls are black and white. Play all day un - til it's night.

ACTIVITY: The Note F (2nd String)

The note on the first space of the staff is called F.

Drawing the Note F

Step 1: Draw an oval notehead on the first space of the staff.

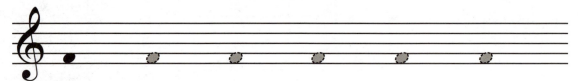

Step 2: For the stem, draw a line from the right of the notehead to the top line of the staff. The stem always goes up for this note.

Now, draw the note F six times below.

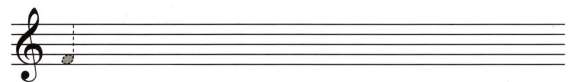

Playing the Note F

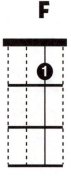

To play the note F, press the 1st fret of the 2nd string.

Indicate the fingering for note F by placing the number "1" in a circle on the 1st fret of the 2nd string on each diagram.

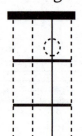 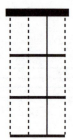 

The Half Rest

Introducing the Half Rest

This rest means do not play for two beats, which is the same as 𝄽 𝄽.

Book 1 — Track 50

Clap and Count out Loud

4/4 ♩ ♩ ♩ ♩ | ♩ ♩ — | ♩ 𝄽 ♩ 𝄽 | — ♩ ♩ ||

1 2 3 4 | 1 2 (3)(4) | 1 (2) 3 (4) | (1)(2) 3 4

(rest)(rest) (rest) (rest)(rest)(rest)

Practice Tip

Notice that the note F and the G⁷ chord are both fingered with finger 1 at the 1st fret on the 2nd string.

In "When I Feel Best," hold the 1st finger down from the third beat of the 1st measure until the last beat of the 5th measure.

Note F

G⁷ Chord

When I Feel Best

Book 1 — Track 51

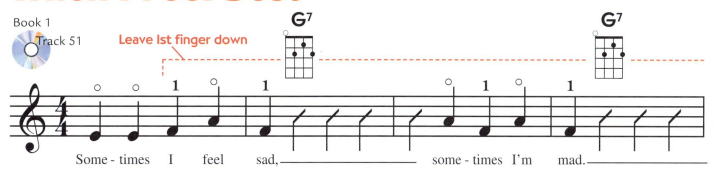

Some-times I feel sad,—— some-times I'm mad.——

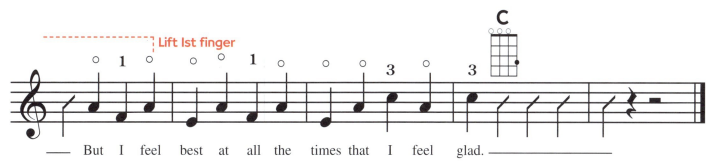

—— But I feel best at all the times that I feel glad.——

57

ACTIVITY: The Half Rest

A *half rest* means do not play for two beats.

How to Draw the Half Rest

Step 1: Draw a box on top of the middle line of the staff.

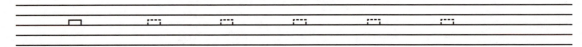

Step 2: Fill in the box.

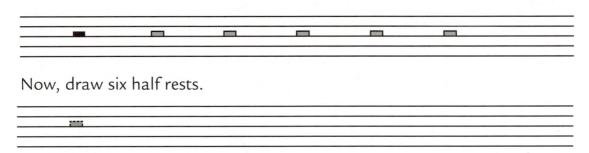

Now, draw six half rests.

Counting Time

Fill in the missing beats with half rests.

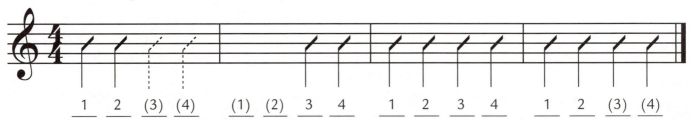

Write the counts for each measure below the quarter-note slashes.

58

Notes on the Second String
Introducing G

Hear this note!
Book 1
Track 52

A note on the 2nd line of the staff is called G. Use finger 3 to press the 2nd string at the 3rd fret. Pick only the 2nd string.

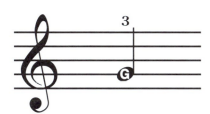

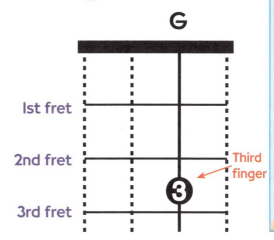

Book 1
Track 53

G Warm-up

A-Choo!

Book 1
Track 54

E and F and G are eas-y. Spil-ling pep-per makes me sneez-y.

"A-a-choo! A-a-choo!" Pep-per makes me go "A-choo!"

ACTIVITY: The Note G (2nd String)

The note on the second line of the staff is called G.

Drawing the Note G

Step 1: Draw an oval notehead on the second line of the staff.

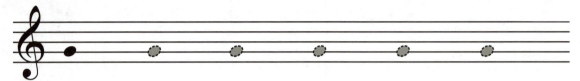

Step 2: For the stem, draw a line from the right of the notehead to just above the top line of the staff. The stem always goes up for this note.

Now, draw the note G six times below.

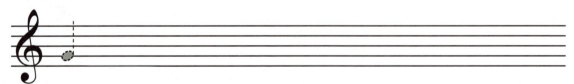

Playing the Note G

To play the note G, press the 3rd fret of the 2nd string.

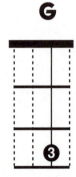

Indicate the fingering for note G by placing the number "3" in a circle on the 3rd fret of the 2nd string on each diagram.

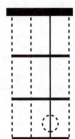
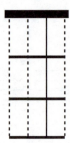

ACTIVITY:
The Notes E, F, G, A, B and C

Reading the Notes E, F, G, A, B, and C

Write the letter name of each note in the box below the staff.

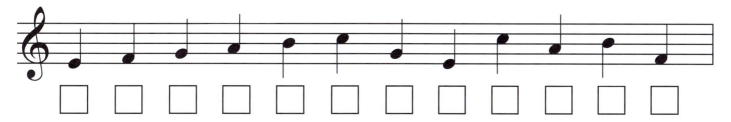

Word Fun with Notes

Write the letter name of each note on the line below the staff. The notes in each measure spell a word!

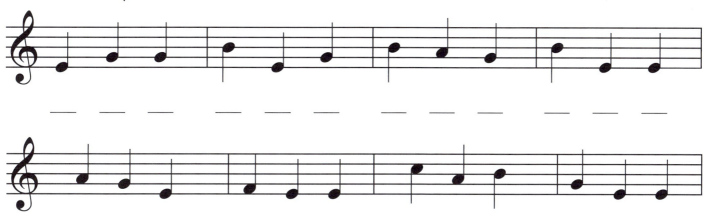

Drawing the Notes E, F, G, A, B, and C

Write the noteheads first, and then add the stems going down.

Now, write all six notes in order from E to C two times.

The Half Note

Introducing the Half Note

𝅗𝅥

2 beats

This note lasts two beats.
It is twice as long as a quarter note.

Book 1
Track 55

Clap and Count out Loud

Hot Cross Buns

Book 1
Track 56

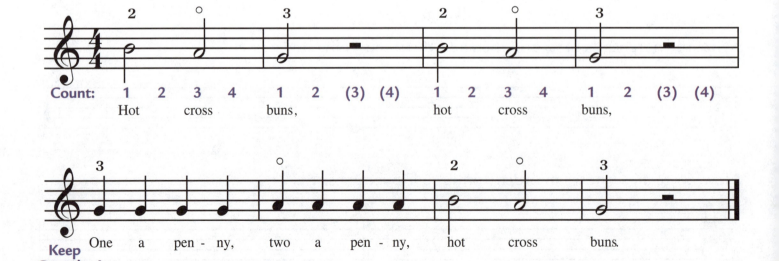

Count: 1 2 3 4 | 1 2 (3) (4) | 1 2 3 4 | 1 2 (3) (4)
Hot cross buns, hot cross buns,

Keep Counting!
One a pen-ny, two a pen-ny, hot cross buns.

ACTIVITY: The Half Note

A *half note* lasts two beats. It is twice as long as a quarter note.

How to Draw the Half Note

Step 1: Create the notehead by drawing an oval. On the staff below, draw three noteheads in the third space and three noteheads in the second space.

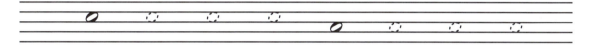

Step 2: Create the stems. For the first three notes, draw the stem going down from the left of the notehead, and for the second three notes, draw the stem going up from the right of the notehead.

Now, draw six half notes. Draw three on the third space, and three on the second space.

Counting Time

Fill in the missing beats by adding either a half rest or a half note in each measure. Then, write the counts below the staff. Put parentheses around beats that are for rests.

63

Notes on the Third String
Introducing C

A line that extends the staff either up or down is called a *ledger line*. A note one ledger line below the staff is called C. You already know C on the 1st string. This C is the open 3rd string and sounds lower than C on the 1st string. To play this note, pick the open 3rd string.

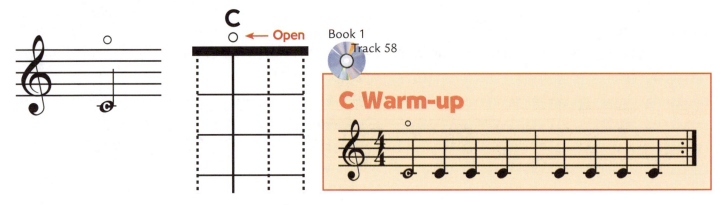

Three Open Strings

Play C o-pen, play E o-pen, play A o-pen, E, C!

Little Steps and Big Leaps

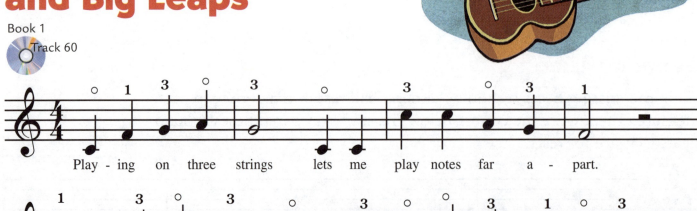

Play-ing on three strings lets me play notes far a-part.

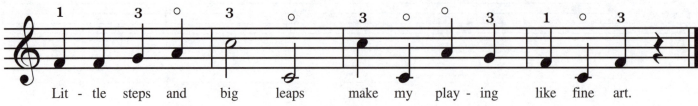

Lit-tle steps and big leaps make my play-ing like fine art.

ACTIVITY: The Note C (3rd String)

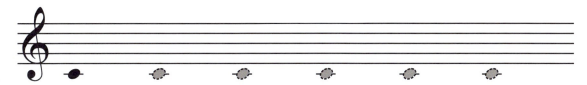

The note on the first ledger line below the staff is called C.

Drawing the Note C

Step 1: Draw an oval notehead on the first ledger line of the staff.

Step 2: For the stem, draw a line from the right of the notehead to just above the third line of the staff. The stem always goes up for this note.

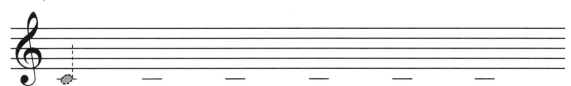

Now, draw the note C six times below.

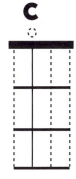

Playing the Note C

To play the note C, pick the open 3rd string.

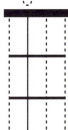

Indicate the fingering for note C by placing "o" above the 3rd string on each diagram.

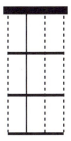
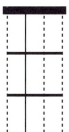

The Old Grey Mare

Book 1
Track 61

(rest) The old grey mare she ain't what she used to be, ain't what she used to be, ain't what she used to be, The old grey mare she ain't what she used to be, man-y long years a-go.

F

Notes on the Third String
Introducing D

Hear this note!
Book 1

Track 62

A note on the space below the staff is called D. Use finger 2 to press the 3rd string at the 2nd fret. Pick only the 3rd string.

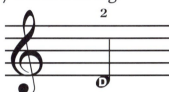

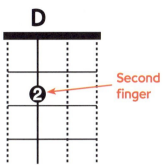

Second finger

Book 1
Track 63

D Warm-up

Introducing the Whole Note

4 beats

This note lasts four beats. It is as long as two half notes, or four quarter notes.

Book 1
Track 64

Clap and Count out Loud
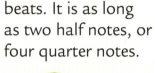

D Is Easy!
Book 1

Track 65

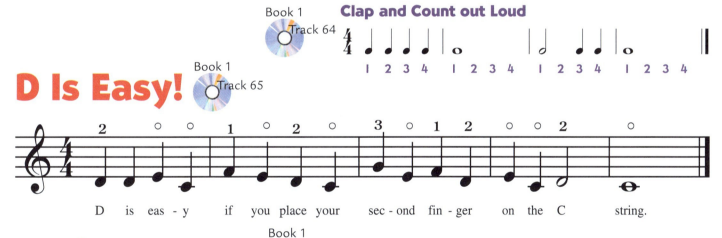

D is eas-y if you place your sec-ond fin-ger on the C string.

Taking a Walk
Book 1
Track 66

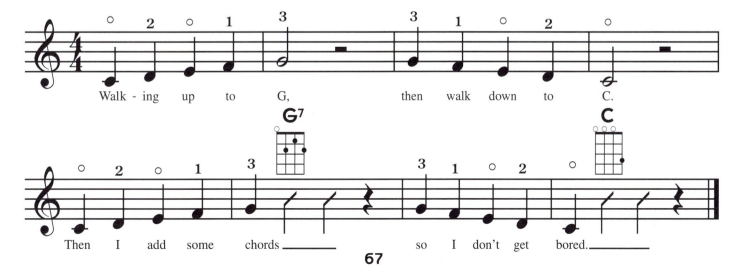

Walk-ing up to G, then walk down to C.
Then I add some chords so I don't get bored.

67

ACTIVITY: The Note D (3rd String)

The note on the first space below the bottom line of the staff is called D.

Drawing the Note D

Step 1: Draw an oval notehead on the space below the bottom line of the staff.

Step 2: For the stem, draw a line from the right of the notehead to the fourth line of the staff. The stem always goes up for this note.

Now, draw the note D six times below.

Playing the Note D

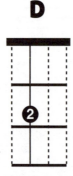

To play the note D, pick the 2nd fret of the 3rd string.

Indicate the fingering for note D by placing the number "2" in a circle on the 2nd fret of the 3rd string on each diagram.

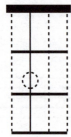 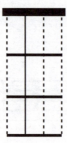 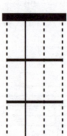

ACTIVITY: The Whole Note

A *whole note* lasts four beats.

How to Draw the Whole Note

Draw an oval in a space or on a line.

Now, draw four whole notes on spaces and four whole notes on lines.

ACTIVITY: Review: All the Notes and Chords in Book I

Write the letter name of each note in the box below the staff.

Write the name of each chord in the box above the chord diagram.

Ode to Joy
from Beethoven's 9th Symphony

Book 1
 Track 67

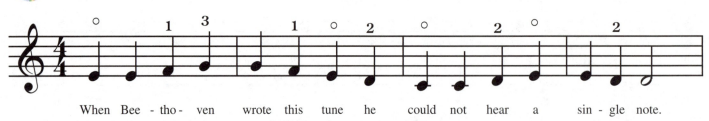

When Bee-tho-ven wrote this tune he could not hear a sin-gle note.

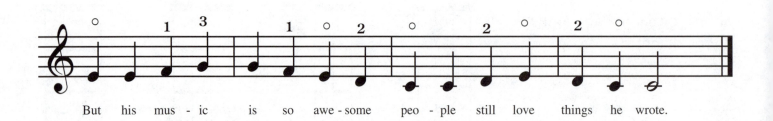

But his mus-ic is so awe-some peo-ple still love things he wrote.

Jingle Bells

Mary Had a Little Lamb

Book 1
Track 69

Ma - ry had a lit - tle lamb, lit - tle lamb, lit - tle lamb,

Ma - ry had a lit - tle lamb, its fleece was white as snow.

Ev - 'ry - where that Ma - ry went, Ma - ry went, Ma - ry went,

Ev - 'ry - where that Ma - ry went, the lamb was sure to go.

Review: Music Matching Games

Chords

Draw a line to match each chord frame on the left to the correct photo on the right.

1.
2.
3.
4.

Symbols

Draw a line to match each symbol on the left to its name on the right.

1. o   Treble clef
2. ♩   Quarter note
3. 𝅗𝅥   Whole note
4. ╱   Quarter slash
5. 𝄞   Half note
6. ‖   Double bar line
7. ▬   Half rest
8. 𝄽   Repeat sign
9. ▬   Quarter rest

Notes

Draw a line to match each note on the left to its correct music notation on the right.

1.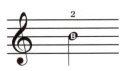
2.
3.
4.
5.
6.
7.
8.

Answer Key

Chords
1: page 23; 2: page 20; 3: page 16; 4: page 31

Symbols
1: page 67; 2: page 62; 3: page 41; 4: page 10;
5: page 39; 6: page 28; 7: page 57; 8: page 18;
9: page 10

Notes
1: page 43; 2: page 46; 3: page 49; 4: page 52;
5: page 55; 6: page 59; 7: page 64; 8: page 67

All the Notes I Know So Far

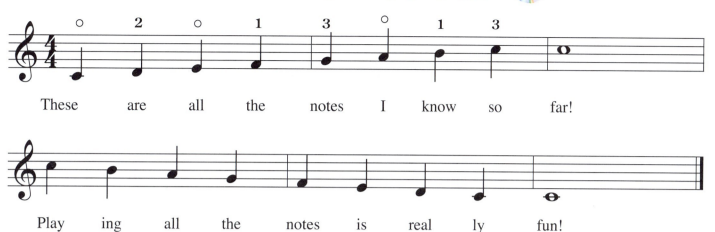

Introducing the Octave

When notes have the same name but one sounds higher or lower, the notes are an octave apart. *Octave* means eight (like octopus with eight legs), so two notes with the same name but are eight notes apart are called an octave.

This Is an Octave

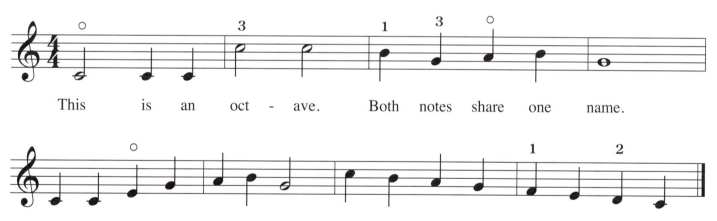

Largo

(from the *New World Symphony*)

This version of composer Antonin Dvořák's famous melody uses all the notes you know so far except one. Which note is missing?

Book 2

Track 5

Antonin Dvořák

Answer: B

Dotted Half Notes & 3/4 Time

The 3/4 Time Signature

Introducing the Dotted Half Note

3 beats

This note looks like a half note, but with a dot to the right of the notehead. It lasts three beats.

A 3/4 time signature ("three-four time") means there are 3 equal beats in every measure.

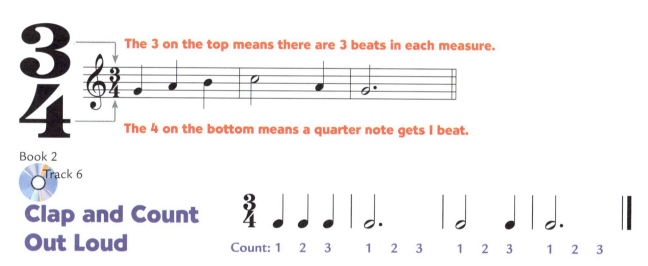

The 3 on the top means there are 3 beats in each measure.

The 4 on the bottom means a quarter note gets 1 beat.

Book 2 Track 6

Clap and Count Out Loud

Count: 1 2 3   1 2 3   1 2 3   1 2 3

Three Is for Me!

Book 2 Track 7

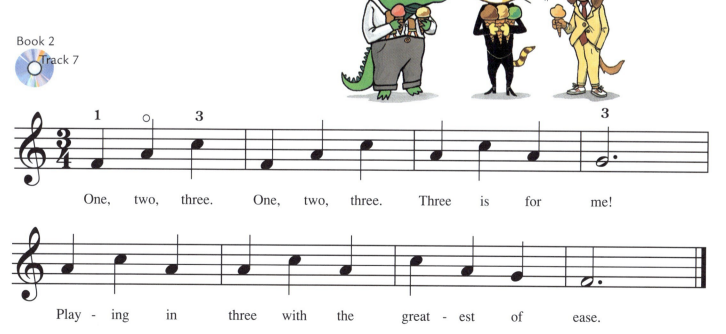

One, two, three. One, two, three. Three is for me!

Play - ing in three with the great - est of ease.

77

ACTIVITY: The Dotted Half Note

The *dotted half note* lasts three beats.

How to Draw the Dotted Half Note

Step 1: Draw a half note.

Step 2: Add a dot to the right of the notehead.

Now, draw three dotted half notes with stems going up and three dotted half notes with stems going down.

ACTIVITY: The 3/4 Time Signature

A 3/4 time signature means there are three equal beats in every measure.

How to Draw the 3/4 Time Signature

Step 1: Draw a number "3" sitting on top of the third line of the staff.

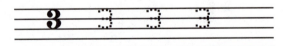

Step 2: Draw a number "4" sitting on the bottom line below the number 3.

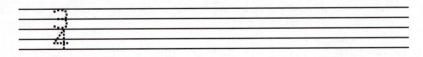

Now, draw six 3/4 time signatures.

The Farmer in the Dell

Book 2 Track 8

Beautiful Brown Eyes

Book 2 Track 9

Beau - ti - ful, beau - ti - ful brown eyes,

smil - ing right in - to my heart. But now

where are those beau - ti - ful brown eyes? Why

must we be so far a - part?

Introducing Common Time C

This symbol is a time signature that means the same as $\frac{4}{4}$.

C = $\frac{4}{4}$ The 4 on the top means there are 4 beats in each measure.
The 4 on the bottom means a quarter note gets 1 beat.

Old MacDonald Had a Farm

Book 2 Track 10

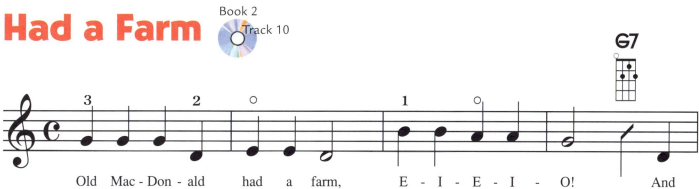

Old Mac-Don-ald had a farm, E - I - E - I - O! And

on that farm he had a uke! E - I - E - I - O!

ACTIVITY: Common Time

This symbol 𝄴 is a time signature that means the same as 4/4 time. There are four beats to each measure.

How to Draw the Common Time Signature

Draw a letter "C" from the fourth line to the second line.

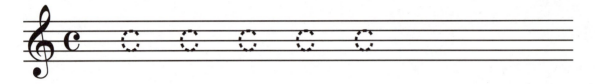

Now, draw six common time signatures.

Choose the Time Signature

Each of the following examples has either three or four beats in each measure. Place either 4/4, 𝄴, or 3/4 at the beginning of each example. Use each time signature only once.

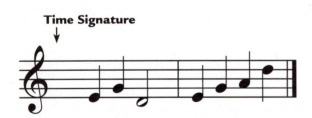

Introducing B-flat

A *flat* ♭ lowers a note a *half step* (the distance from one fret to another is called a half step). B♭ is played one fret lower than the note B. When a flat note appears in a measure, it is still flat until the end of that measure.

Hear this note! Book 2 Track 11

1st FRET

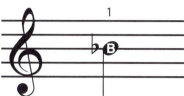

Aura Lee

Book 2 Track 12

Elvis Presley recorded this folk song as a pop ballad called "Love Me Tender."

New Note B♭

ACTIVITY: The Note B-flat

The note on the middle line of the staff with a flat ♭ symbol before it is called B♭.

Drawing the Note B-flat

To draw the note B♭ on the staff, place the notehead on the third line, and draw the stem down to just below the staff. Then draw a small lower case "b" just to the left of the notehead. On the staff below, draw the note B♭ six times.

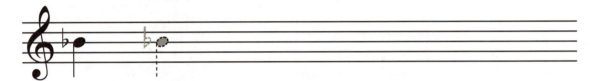

Playing the Note B♭

To play the note B♭, press the 1st string at the 1st fret.

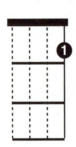

On the diagram to the right, indicate the fingering for the note B♭ by placing the number "1" in a circle on the 1st fret of the 1st string.

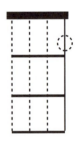

Write Your Own Song with the Notes C, D, E, F, G, A, B-flat and C

Compose a short melody with the notes C, D, E, F, G, A, B-flat, and C. Use quarter notes, half notes, dotted half notes, and whole notes. Remember that in 4/4 time, only four beats fit in each measure.

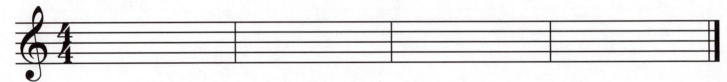

Three-String Boogie

Book 2
Track 13

This song uses all the notes you have learned. Don't forget to listen to the audio recording first!

Tempo Signs

A *tempo sign* tells you how fast to play the music. Below are the three most common tempo signs.

Andante ("ahn-DAHN-teh") **slow**

Moderato ("moh-deh-RAH-toh") **moderately**

Allegro ("ah-LAY-groh") **fast**

Three-Tempo Rock

Play three times: first time **Andante**, second time **Moderato**, third time **Allegro**.

Andante — Book 2 Track 14   Moderato — Book 2 Track 15   Allegro — Book 2 Track 16

Count: 1 2 3 (rest)

Writing Tempo Signs

Write the correct tempo sign next to the speed that matches.

slow _____   moderately _____   fast _____

Rockin' Uke

Book 2
Track 17

Good Night Ladies

Book 2 Track 18 Vocals & Chords   Book 2 Track 19 Chords Only

For this song and most of the rest of the songs in this book, you can play either the melody or chords. Your teacher can play the part you aren't playing, or you can play along with the recording.

Moderato

Good night, la - dies, Good night, la - dies,

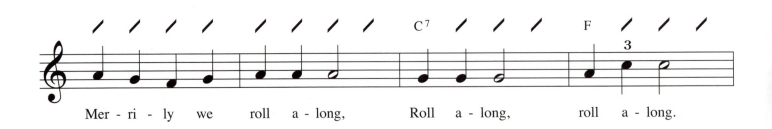

Good night, la - dies, We're going to leave you now.

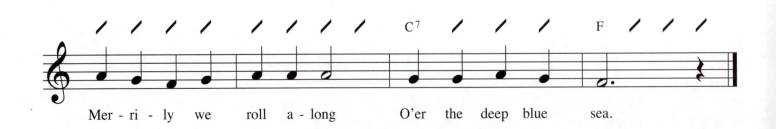

Mer - ri - ly we roll a - long, Roll a - long, roll a - long.

Mer - ri - ly we roll a - long O'er the deep blue sea.

Blues in C

Ties

A *tie* is a curved line that connects two of the same note. When two notes are tied, don't play the second note, but keep the first note playing until the second note is done. You are really adding the two notes together.

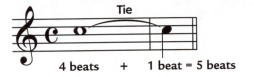

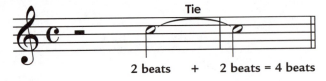

Clap and Count Out Loud

Book 2
Track 21

Down in the Valley

Book 2
Track 22
Vocals & Chords

Book 2
Track 23
Chords Only

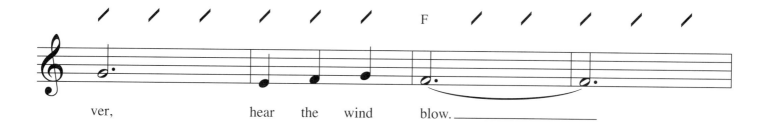
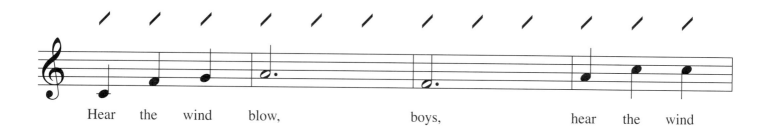
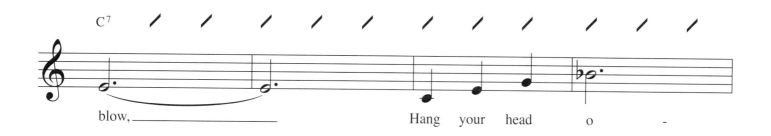
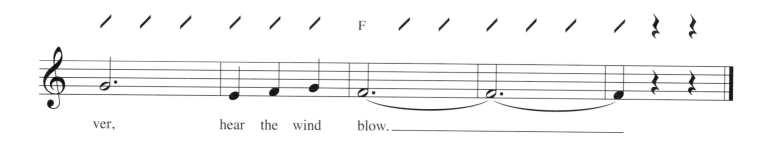

91

ACTIVITY: Ties

A *tie* is a curved line that connects two of the same note. When two notes are tied, don't play the second note, but add the two notes together instead.

How to Draw the Tie

When the notes being tied are on or above the middle line of the staff, the curve of the tie goes up.

When the notes being tied are below the middle line of the staff, the curve of the tie goes down.

Draw ties to connect the notes below. Then write the total number of beats for each pair on the line below the staff.

5 beats

_____

_____

_____

_____

_____

Key Signatures

The *key signature* at the beginning of a piece tells you when a note is played as a flat note throughout the piece. In "Ode to Joy," each B is played as B-flat.

Ode to Joy (Extended Version)

Book 2

Track 24
Vocals & Chords

Book 2
Track 25
Chords Only

Key Signature: remember to play each B one half step lower.

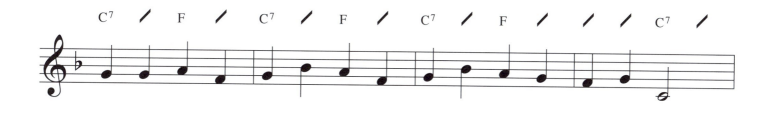

ACTIVITY: Key Signatures

The key signature at the beginning of a piece of music tells you when a note is played as a flat note throughout the piece.

In "Ode to Joy" below, draw a blue box around all the B-flats that are on beat two of a measure, and draw a red box around all the B-flats that are on beat three.

Ode to Joy

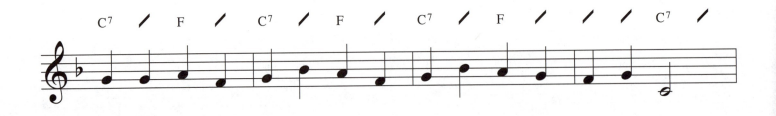

Pickup Measures

Not all pieces of music begin on the first beat. Sometimes music begins with just part of a measure, which is called a *pickup*.

A pickup is like a pumpkin pie. If you were to cut the pie into four equal pieces and take one piece away, there would be three pieces left. If you are playing in 4/4 time and the pickup measure has one quarter note, there will be three quarter notes in the last measure.

Playing in 3/4 time is like cutting the pie into three equal pieces: if there is one quarter note as a pickup, there will be two quarter notes in the last measure.

Clap and Count Out Loud Book 2 Track 26

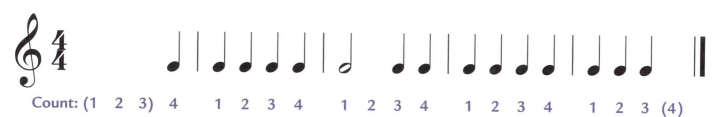

Count: (1 2 3) 4   1 2 3 4   1 2 3 4   1 2 3 4   1 2 3 (4)

A-Tisket, A-Tasket

Book 2 Track 27 Vocals & Chords   Book 2 Track 28 Chords Only

95

ACTIVITY: Pickup Measures

Counting Time

For each example, write the counts for the pickup measure and the final measure under the staff. Put parentheses around the counts that aren't played.

Tom Dooley

Book 2
Track 29
Vocals & Chords

Book 2
Track 30
Chords Only

Moderately slow

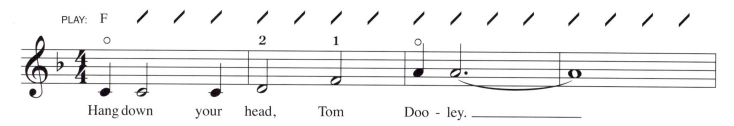

Hang down your head, Tom Doo - ley.

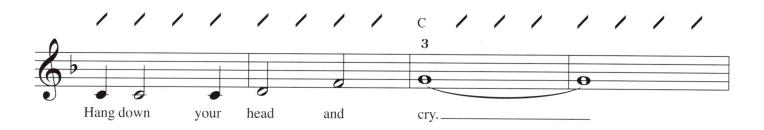

Hang down your head and cry.

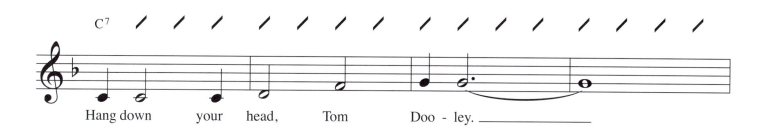

Hang down your head, Tom Doo - ley.

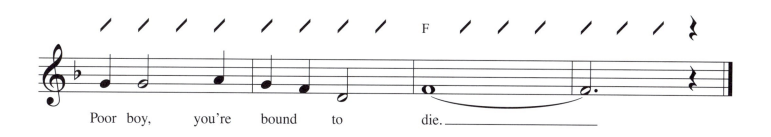

Poor boy, you're bound to die.

Eighth Notes

Eighth notes are black notes with a flag added to the stem: ♪ or ♪.
Two or more eighth notes are written with beams: ♫ or ♫, ♬ or ♬.
Each eighth note receives one half beat.

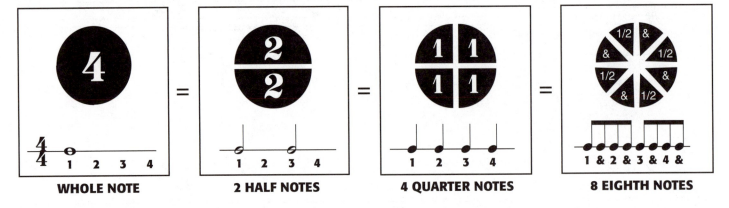

Use alternating downstrokes ⊓ and upstrokes V on eighth notes.

Book 2 Track 31

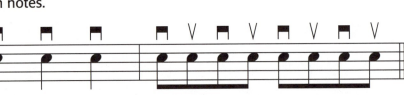

Jammin' with Eighth Notes

Book 2 Track 32 Melody & Chords Book 2 Track 33 Chords Only

Allegro moderato*

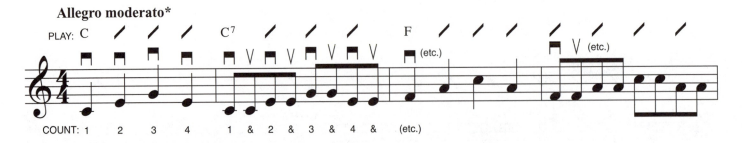

*Allegro moderato means moderately fast.

98

ACTIVITY: The Eighth Note

An *eighth note* has a black notehead, a stem, and a flag. Each eighth note equals ½ beat.

How to Draw the Eighth Note

Step 1: Draw a quarter note.

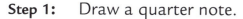

Step 2: Draw the flag up from the bottom of the stem that look like the leaf of a flower..

Now, draw six eighth notes on the third space of the staff.

Now, draw six eighth notes in the second space with the stem going up from the right of the notehead, and the flag going down instead of up.

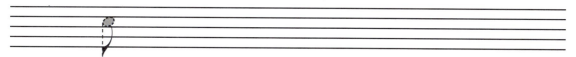

Beaming Eighth Notes

Draw eight eighth notes in each measure and beam the notes in groups of four (♫♫). In the first measure, draw eighth notes having stems down, and in the second measure, draw eighth notes having stems up. Then, write the counts below the staff.

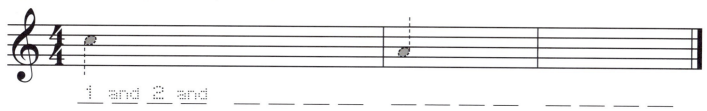

1 and 2 and

Go Tell Aunt Rhody

Book 2 — Track 34 Vocals & Chords
Book 2 — Track 35 Chords Only

Moderato

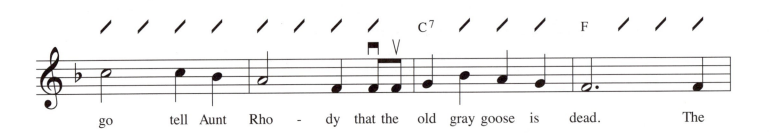

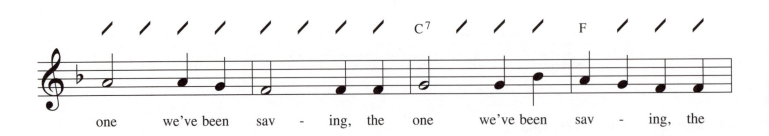

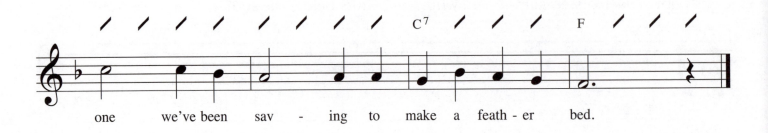

Love Somebody (Extended Version)

Book 2
Track 36
Vocals & Chords

Book 2
Track 37
Chords Only

Moderately

Love some-bod-y, yes, I do; Love some-bod-y, yes, I do;

Love some-bod-y, yes, I do; Love some-bod-y, but I won't tell who.

Love some-bod-y, yes, I do; Love some-bod-y, yes, I do;

Love some-bod-y, yes, I do; And I hope some-bod-y loves me too.

Clementine

Book 2
Track 38
Vocals & Chords

Book 2
Track 39
Chords Only

Moderately fast

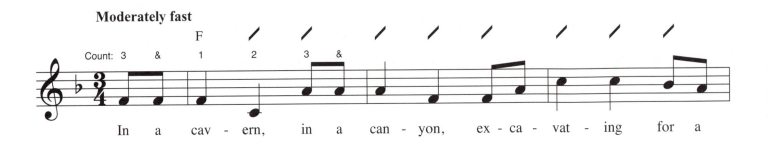

In a cav-ern, in a can-yon, ex-ca-vat-ing for a

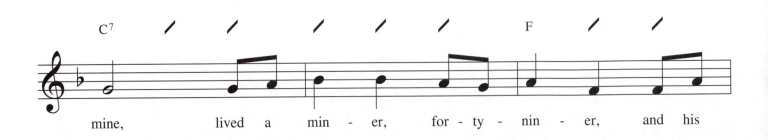

mine, lived a min-er, for-ty-nin-er, and his

daugh-ter, Clem-en-tine. Oh my dar-lin', oh my

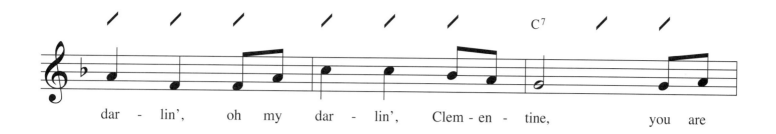

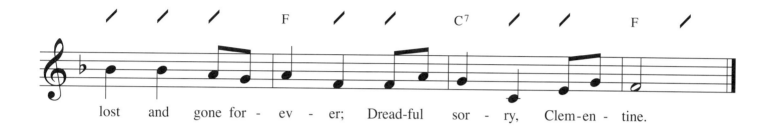

Additional Verses

Verse 2:
Light she was and like a fairy,
And her shoes were number nine,
Herring boxes, without topses,
Sandals were for Clementine.

Chorus:
Oh my darlin', oh my darlin',
Oh my darlin' Clementine!
You art lost and gone forever
Dreadful sorry, Clementine.

Verse 3:
Drove she ducklings to the water
Every morning just at nine,
Hit her foot against a splinter,
Fell into the foaming brine.

Chorus:
Oh my darlin', oh my darlin',
Oh my darlin' Clementine!
You art lost and gone forever
Dreadful sorry, Clementine.

Verse 4:
Ruby lips above the water,
Blowing bubbles soft and fine,
But, alas, I was no swimmer,
So I lost my Clementine.

Chorus:
Oh my darlin', oh my darlin',
Oh my darlin' Clementine!
You art lost and gone forever
Dreadful sorry, Clementine.

Dotted Quarter Notes

A DOT INCREASES THE LENGTH OF A NOTE BY ONE HALF

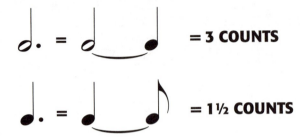

Counting Dotted Quarter Notes

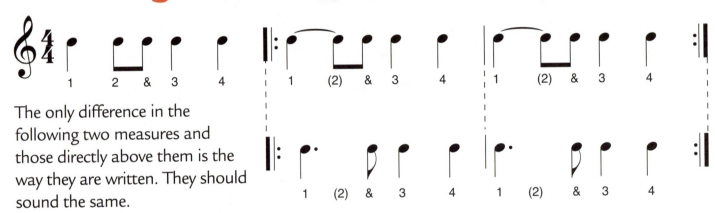

The only difference in the following two measures and those directly above them is the way they are written. They should sound the same.

Cockles and Mussels

Book 2 Track 40 Vocals & Chords
Book 2 Track 41 Chords Only

Moderately

In Dub-lin's fair cit-y, where girls are so pret-ty, I

first set my eyes on sweet Mol-ly Ma-lone, As she

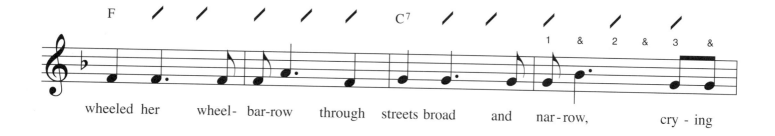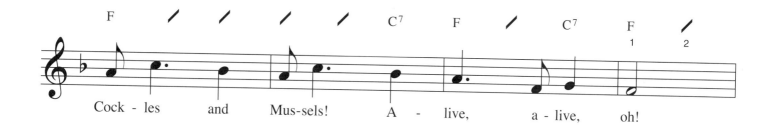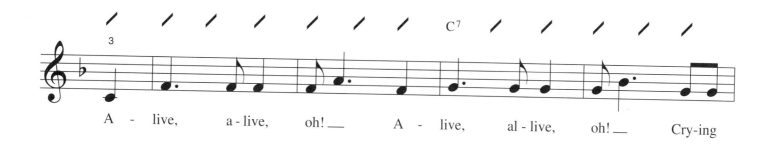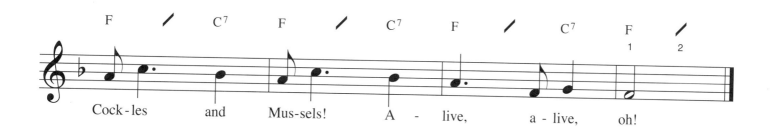

ACTIVITY: The Dotted Quarter Note

The *dotted quarter note* lasts 1 ½ beats.

How to Draw the Dotted Quarter Note

Step 1: Draw a quarter note.

Step 2: Add a dot to the right of the notehead.

Now, draw three dotted quarter notes with stems going up and three dotted quarter notes with stems going down.

Write the Number of Beats

Here are all the types of notes, slashes, and rests you know so far. Write the number of beats each symbol receives (1, 2, 3, 4, one half, or 1 ½) on the line below the staff.

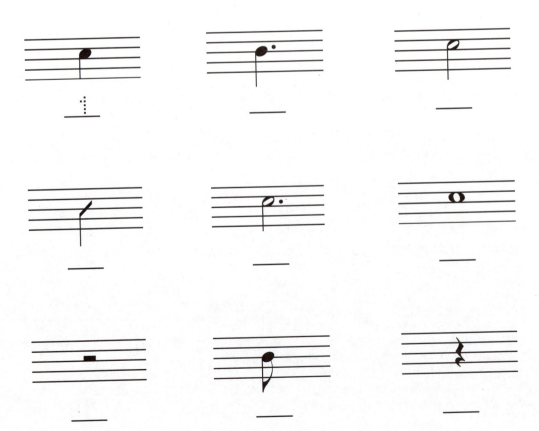

Dynamics

Symbols that show how loud or soft to play are called *dynamics*. These symbols come from Italian words. Four of the most common dynamics are shown here.

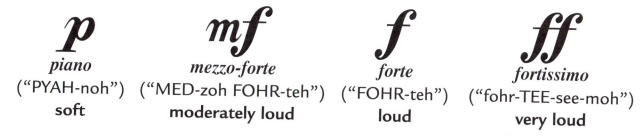

p	**mf**	**f**	**ff**
piano	*mezzo-forte*	*forte*	*fortissimo*
("PYAH-noh")	("MED-zoh FOHR-teh")	("FOHR-teh")	("fohr-TEE-see-moh")
soft	moderately loud	loud	very loud

Echo Rock

Book 2 Track 42 Melody & Chords
Book 2 Track 43 Chords Only

107

The Streets of Laredo

Book 2
Track 44
Vocals & Chords

Book 2
Track 45
Chords Only

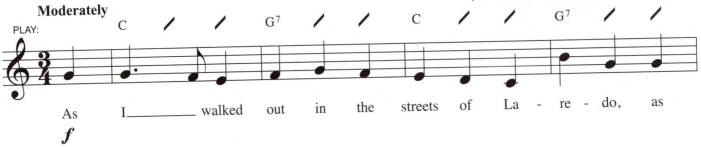

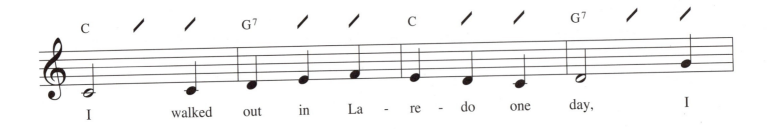

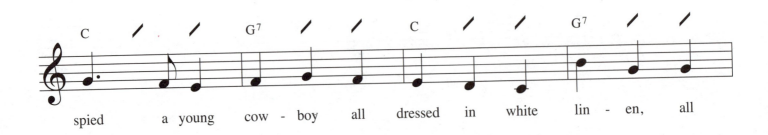

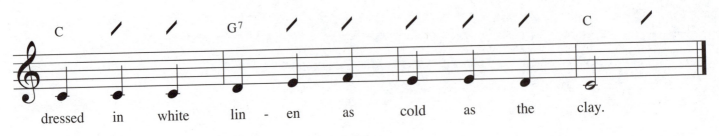

The Down-and-Up Stroke

Book 2
Track 46

You can make your accompaniment of waltz songs in 3/4 like "The Streets of Laredo" more interesting by replacing the second beat of the measure with a downstroke followed by an upstroke. The symbol for downstroke is ⊓; an upstroke uses the symbol V. Together, the down-and-up strokes are two eighth notes that are played in the same time as single quarter note.

Try the following exercise to first just work on the new rhythm.

Now practice changing from C to G7.

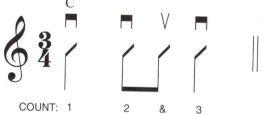

Now practice changing back and forth from C to G7 and back. When you can do it smoothly, go back to page 31 and use it to accompany "The Streets of Laredo."

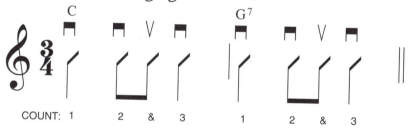

In 4/4 time, use the pattern 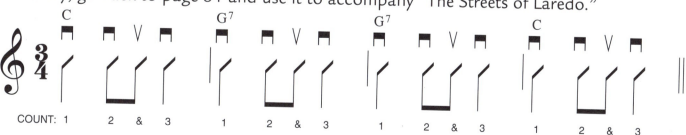.

109

ACTIVITY: Dynamics

Dynamics are symbols that tell you how loud or soft to play. Below are the four most common dynamics.

p stands for *piano*, which means **soft**.

mf stands for *mezzo-forte*, which means **moderately loud**.

f stands for *forte*, which means **loud**.

ff stands for *fortissimo*, which means **very loud**.

Writing Dynamics

Write the correct dynamic sign next to its definition.

loud _____
soft _____
very loud _____
moderately loud _____

ACTIVITY: The Downstroke and Upstroke

Draw the symbol for the downstroke ⊓ six times above these notes.

Draw the symbol for the upstroke V six times above these notes.

The Fermata

This sign is called a *fermata*. It means to hold the note it is over a little longer.

Michael, Row the Boat Ashore

Moderately slow and steady

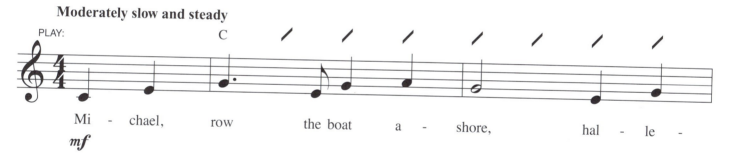

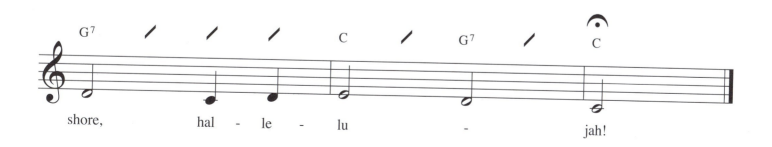

ACTIVITY: The Fermata

A *fermata* means to play the note a little longer than normal (usually about twice the normal length). The fermata is sometimes called a "bird's eye."

Drawing the Fermata

Step 1: Draw the top half of a circle above the note.

Step 2: Place a dot inside the half circle.

Now, draw a fermata over each of the notes below.

Introducing F-sharp

A *sharp* ♯ raises a note a half step. F♯ is played one fret higher than the note F. When a sharp note appears in a measure, it is still sharp until the end of that measure.

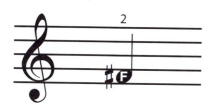

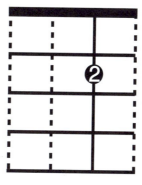

Little Brown Jug

ACTIVITY: The Note F-sharp

The note with a sharp sign on the bottom space of the staff is called F♯.

Drawing the Note F-sharp

To draw the note F♯ on the staff, place the notehead in the bottom space, and draw the stem up to the top line. Then draw a sharp sign ♯ to the left of the notehead. A sharp sign is like a small tic-tac-toe symbol. On the staff below, draw the note F♯ six times.

Playing the Note F♯

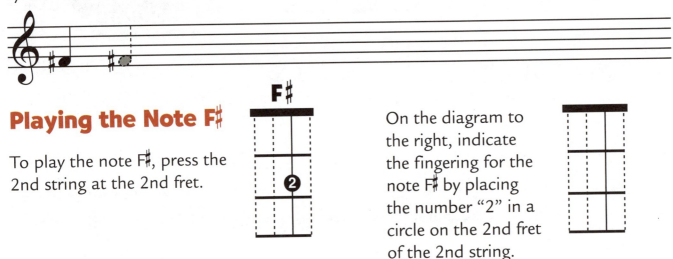

To play the note F♯, press the 2nd string at the 2nd fret.

On the diagram to the right, indicate the fingering for the note F♯ by placing the number "2" in a circle on the 2nd fret of the 2nd string.

Write Your Own Melody with the Notes C, D, E, F-sharp, G, A, B, and C

Compose a short melody with the notes C, D, E, F-sharp, G, A, B, and C. Use eighth notes, quarter notes, dotted quarter notes, half notes, dotted half notes, and whole notes. Also included dynamics and a tempo sign. Remember that in $\frac{4}{4}$ time, only four beats fit in each measure.

The G Chord

Hear this chord! Book 2 Track 52

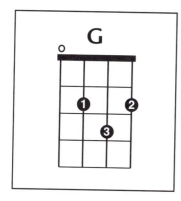

Place your 1st, 2nd, and 3rd fingers in position, then play one string at a time.

Play all four strings together:

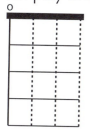 + 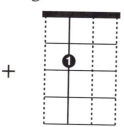 + 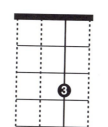 +  =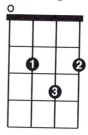

G Chord

The D7 Chord

Hear this chord! Book 2 Track 53

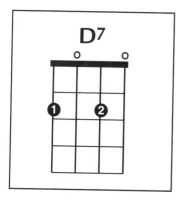

Place your 1st and 2nd fingers in position, then play one string at a time.

Play all four strings together:

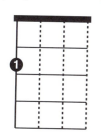 + 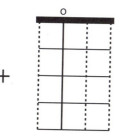 + 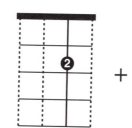 +  =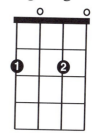

Over the Rainbow (Extended Version)

The greatest ukulele version of this song was recorded in 1993 by legendary Hawaiian uke player and singer Iz.

Book 2 Track 54

Words by E. Y. Harburg
Music by Harold Arlen

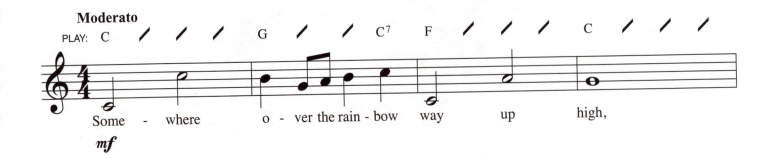

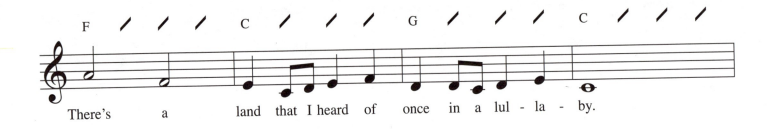

© 1938 (Renewed) METRO-GOLDWYN-MAYER INC.
© 1939 (Renewed) EMI FEIST CATALOG INC.
Rights throughout the World Controlled by EMI FEIST CATALOG INC. (Publishing) and ALFRED MUSIC PUBLISHING CO., INC. (Print)
All Rights Reserved

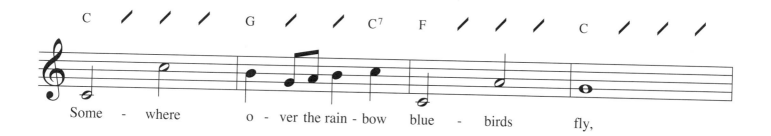
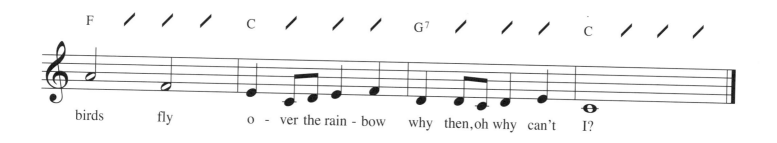

ACTIVITY: The G and D7 Chords

The G Chord

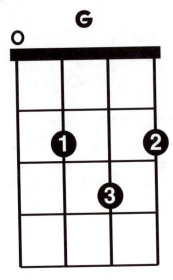

Write the chord symbol "G" three times.

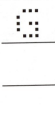

_____

_____

The D7 Chord

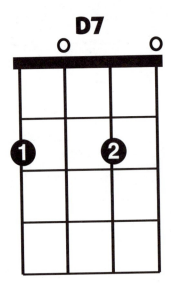

Write the chord symbol "D7" three times.

_____

_____

Finish drawing the **o**'s and fingering for the chords below.

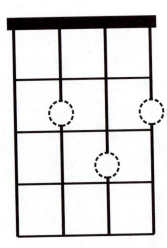
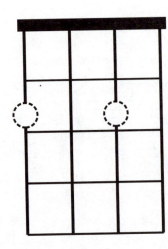

ACTIVITY:
Review: All the Notes and Chords You Learned

Write the letter name of each note in the box below the staff.

Write the name of each chord in the box above the chord diagram.

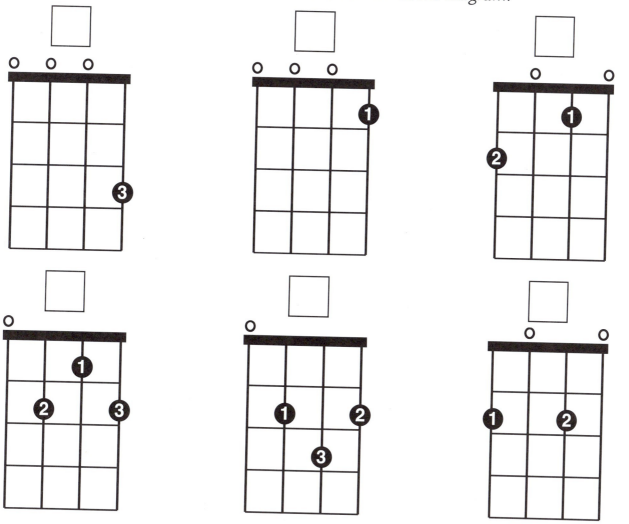

Review: Music Matching Games

Chords — Draw a line to match each chord frame on the left to the correct photo on the right.

1. F
2. C7
3. C
4. G7
5. G
6. D7

Symbols — Draw a line to match each symbol on the left to its name on the right.

1.   Dotted half note
2.   Whole rest
3.  Tie
4. *ff* Three beats in a measure
5. — Fermata
6. *Moderato* Common time
7. *mf* Loud
8. **C** Moderately Loud
9. *Allegro* Soft
10. *p* Very loud
11. *Andante* Slow
12.   Moderately
13. *f* Fast

Notes — Draw a line to match each note on the left to its correct music notation on the right.

1.
2.
3.
4.
5.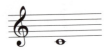
6.
7.
8.
9.
10.

Answer Key

Chords
1: page 23; 2: page 20; 3: page 16; 4: page 31; 5: page 115; 6: page 115

Symbols
1: page 90; 2: page 77; 3: page 77; 4: page 107; 5: page 57; 6: page 86; 7: page 107; 8: page 81; 9: page 86; 10: page 107; 11: page 86; 12: page 111; 13: page 107

Notes
1: page 49; 2: page 52; 3: page 43; 4: page 68; 5: page 55; 6: page 59; 7: page 46; 8: page 64; 9: page 83; 10: page 113;